EYLIANA and IKEY

E C I

COHEN

WEDDING OF
IKEY AND EYLIANA COHEN
03.09.21

consciously

consciously

SIX STEPS TO LIVING VIBRANTLY
WITH OUR CREATOR

MENACHEM POZNANSKI , LCSW
WITH FOREWORD BY RABBI JOEY ROSENFELD

Copyright © 2020 by Mosaica Press

ISBN: 978-1-952370-09-0

All rights reserved. No part of this book may be used or reproduced or transmitted in any form or by any means, electronic or mechanical, including photocopying, recording, or by any information storage and retrieval system, without written permission from the publisher.

Published by Mosaica Press, Inc.
www.mosaicapress.com
info@mosaicapress.com

In loving memory of
our father, grandfather,
and great-grandfather

POPPY
Irwin S. Friedman
Yisroel Izaak ben Menachem

Who survived the horrors of the Nazi nightmare and went on, together with his wife, our beloved Edith (Momma) Friedman, to raise and nurture a loving family, and live a truly full and successful life.

His loving daughter
LYNN FRIEDMAN AND FAMILY

In loving memory of

Jack Genauer
יעקב קעפל בן משה יהודה הלוי

A warm and loving grandfather who cherished his family and always had a smile for everyone. Charismatic and inherently proud to be a Jew, his legacy as a role-model and a community leader continues to inspire us.

יהי זכרו ברוך

His loving grandson
AKIVA AND MIMI FRIEND AND FAMILY

Benjamin Epstein, Ph.D.

The notion of separation in spirituality is not one of physical distance but rather a matter of degree and levels. There is no rocket ship to take to get "there"—it is not somewhere over the rainbow. To be "close" to Hashem requires an expanded awareness to the divinity imbued in every moment and within ourselves. "For it is within your close reach to follow the Torah in speech, feeling, and deed." When we become stuck in physical space and the world of time, then the God of our understanding can become distant, cold, and even absent. In this beautiful offering, an integration of the author's clinical acumen, along with the roadmap provided by the works of the *Bilvavi Mishkan Evneh*, the wisdom of the 12 Steps and the enlivening teachings of our Captain Rav Moshe Weinberger, *shlita*, Reb Menachem has attempted to deftly teach the spiritual seeker how to attach oneself through conscious contact with our Creator. If you feel the purpose of your life is to bond yourself to the ultimate good, then *Consciously* can help serve as an ever-present reminder that the Goal is Soul.

Benjamin Epstein, Ph.D.,
author of *Living in the Presence:
A Jewish Mindfulness Guide to Everyday Life*

RABBI EFREM GOLDBERG
BOCA RATON SYNAGOGUE

הרב אפרים חיים גולדברג
ק"ק בית כנסת בוקא ראטון

בס"ד

July 1, 2020
8 Tamuz, 5780

While many who crave a relationship with Hashem study about Him, few succeed to live with Him. Often a barrier to palpably feeling Hashem's presence and His love is the feeling of inadequacy or unworthiness to share a closeness with the Master of the Universe.

In this outstanding work, Menachem Poznanski reminds us that, in fact, Hashem can be found in our imperfection, our struggles and even our failures, as long as we live consciously and attach ourselves to Him. In Consciously, which is simultaneously profound and yet refreshingly practical, Menachem communicates the timeless wisdom of Torah and the principles of the Bilvavi Mishkan Evneh through the contemporary language and examples gleaned from his extensive experience as a clinician and therapist.

If you want to learn to not only talk about Hashem, but to hear Him talking to you and to genuinely talk with Him, Menachem's guide is an indispensable tool.

החותם בידידות ובברכה,

Congregation Aish Kodesh
of Woodmere
351 Midwood Road
Woodmere, N. Y. 11598
516 - 569-2660
—
RABBI MOSHE WEINBERGER

קהילת אש קודש דוודמיר

הרב משה וויינבערגער
מרא דאתרא

ב"ה

ב' תמוז תש"פ

    My dear friend Menachem Poznanski has crafted another masterpiece. "Consciously" is a breathtakingly clear and practical guide to developing an authentic relationship with Hashem. Based upon the revolutionary sefer Bilvavi Mishkan Evneh by HaRav Itamar Schwartz, R. Menachem literally takes the reader by the hand to lead him/her down the pathways of Kirvas Hashem in a healthy, down to earth way. By combining his vast clinical knowledge and experience together with the ancient and ever relevant teachings of Torah, R. Menachem has authored a truly groundbreaking manual for spiritual development. "Taste and you shall see."

בצפי'ה לראות בהרמת קרן התורה ועובדת הבורא

Table of Contents

Acknowledgments XV
Foreword XX
Introduction 1

step one
Primary Spiritual Purpose

CHAPTER 1
The Importance of Knowing One's Purpose. 19

CHAPTER 2
Missing the Forest for All the Trees. 22

CHAPTER 3
Individual Mission and Fundamental Mission. 27

CHAPTER 4
What Is Our Primary Spiritual Purpose? 33

INTO ACTION—STEP 1
Primary Spiritual Purpose. 42

step two
Consciousness of Contact

CHAPTER 5
What Is Closeness to G-d?. 47

XII *Consciously*

CHAPTER 6
Is Wholesome Completeness Really Possible? 51

INTO ACTION—STEP 2
Consciousness of Contact 60

step three
Willingness to Connect

CHAPTER 7
Do I Actually Want Conscious Contact? 67

CHAPTER 8
Prayer I: Praying for Willingness 72

INTO ACTION—STEP 3
Willingness to Connect 78

step four
There Is a Creator

CHAPTER 9
Keep It Simple: Awareness of a Creator 85

CHAPTER 10
Like You Won the Lottery:
   "There's Knowing and Then There's KNOWING" . . . 91

CHAPTER 11
Tasting G-d 95

CHAPTER 12
Transforming Our Hearts 100

INTO ACTION—STEP 4
Meet Our Creator 108

step five
Connect with Createdness

CHAPTER 13
A Fully Practical Spirituality 113

CHAPTER 14
Inner Pharaoh—Guerilla Warrior 121

CHAPTER 15
Recognizing Our Createdness—Revealing Inner Abraham. 125

INTO ACTION—STEP 5
Connect with Createdness. 130

step six
G-d Is in Charge

CHAPTER 16
How "In Charge" Is G-d? 143

CHAPTER 17
Transforming Our Hearts: Spiritual Speech. 147

CHAPTER 18
Anger, Frustration, and Resentment. 153

CHAPTER 19
G-d's Way or My Way: Inner Bilaam 158

CHAPTER 20
Seeing through the Creator's Eyes 167

CHAPTER 21
Prayer II: A World of Prayer 173

XIV *Consciously*

INTO ACTION—STEP 6
G-d Is in Charge 181

Action: An Epilogue 189

Acknowledgments

MY PERSONAL JOURNEY toward this publication began over fifteen years ago, when I was introduced to the classes of Rav Moshe Weinberger, *shlita*, on what was then a new literary work titled *Bilvavi Mishkan Evneh*. As you will read in the pages to come, concepts from *Bilvavi* (as it is commonly known) form the basis of everything we will discuss here. Hearing those classes was my first real exposure to Rav Weinberger, a teacher who has since influenced and shaped my perspective and understanding of Judaism in particular and spirituality in general. In these classes, Rav Weinberger described a revolution of Jewish thought that wasn't really a revolution at all, because the principles it put forward lay at the ancient foundation of the inner world of Torah. These teachings brought to the fore a comprehensive action plan for developing something that I, for so long, had wanted, but didn't have any hope of ever achieving: a vibrant relationship with G-d. Hearing the classes and studying the text quite literally changed my life. For that reason, the fact that Rav Weinberger himself was willing to review *Consciously* and provide an approbation is the greatest honor. I am so thankful to you, Rebbe. I also want to acknowledge the author of *Bilvavi*, Rav Itamar Schwartz, *shlita*. Rav Schwartz initially published *Bilvavi* anonymously, but as time went on, his identity was uncovered and he went on to became the leader he is today. *Bilvavi*, *Chelek Aleph* (Part 1) and the volumes that followed have become incredibly popular in Israel and all over the world. I therefore begin by acknowledging the infinite gift that these two great lights have brought to my life. This book would be completely and utterly impossible without these two great men.

Next: acknowledgment of the influence, support, and encouragement I have received from my friends/mentors. There are many, but I thought it pertinent to name a few specifically. The first of these is someone who has been a confidante and guide for nearly twenty years, R' Yudy Wiener. Yudy was the first to introduce me to the world of chassidus in general, and *Bilvavi* specifically, at a time when I had lost hope of ever finding spiritual comfort. I will never be able to fully repay the kindness he has shown me and my family. I also want to thank R' Mayer Preger, who introduced me, in earnest, to the world of Chabad Chassidus, specifically the teachings of the Alter Rebbe of Chabad in *Tanya*, and of the Rebbe, of blessed memory. The influence of the *Tanya* on my entire outlook and perspective is absolute. Everything I study and all of my practice is seen through the lens of *Tanya*. I also want to acknowledge Rabbi Chaim Glancz, the head and heart of Our Place in NY, a treasured mentor and friend. I also want to take this opportunity to acknowledge and thank HaGaon HaRav Binyamin Moskowitz and HaRav Mordechai Sher, my early teachers.

Finally, in this sphere, I want to acknowledge and thank my friend and teacher Rabbi Joey Rosenfeld. Joey and I have known each other for nearly twenty years, and it has been my pleasure and honor to watch him grow into the man he is today. More recently, Joey has become a treasured teacher, as he spills forth a wellspring of wisdom and insight that is precious and critical. I cannot properly express the extent to which Rav Joey's encouragement, input and support has made this project possible. It is my great honor, and it is only befitting, that he reviewed the material as a content editor and wrote the foreword for *Consciously*. I am eternally grateful to him for this, for his friendship, and for what I have learned from him over the past few years. On that note, I also want to express my deepest thanks to Rabbi Efrem Goldberg and Dr. Ben Epstein, who agreed to review the material and provide letters of approbation. It is my great honor to have your encouragement in this process. I also want to thank Rabbi

Doron Kornbluth, Rabbi Haber, and the entire Mosaica Press team, who did such a remarkable job taking a simple manuscript and transforming it into a book worth reading.

Giving thanks on a personal level is challenging, as there are so many people I want to thank—too many to name. There are friends with whom I have had the pleasure to review this material, fellows who gave me encouragement and support, and countless people that have shared with me their own journey in a way that inspired me to continue mine. Though you remain anonymous, I thank each and every one of you—you know who you are. Specifically, though, I want to thank my colleagues at Our Place/The Living Room: Benjy Berger, Trish Attia, the entire Our Place board, Yossie Yurowitz, Eli Vershalizer, Rabbi Zvi Gluck, and Rabbi Aryeh Young. Most precious to acknowledge is my TLR team: Gittel Follman, Miriam Bracha Handelsman, Shmaya Honickman, Yosef Nissanian, Esti Heller, Eta Bienenstock, and Chaim Kohn. In particular, Chaim and Shmaya, who joined me in the journey of putting these teachings down into audio form on a podcast. I also want to express my love and affection to the entire TLR Family: I love you all! I want to give special mention to my dear friend and brother Mr. Akiva Friend and his wife Mimi, who were major sponsors for *Consciously* and are always close to our heart. Finally, in the friend zone, I could never skip Aryeh Buchsbayew, my partner in our last book. Aryeh is a constant companion and confidante in my work as a clinician.

This year I had a great gift. I began to study *Bilvavi* with my daughter Zoe. This has been a great and awesome thrill for me, to draw this text into the sphere of my inner circle. My family members—my wife Naomi, our children Zoe and Tani, our parents, our siblings, nieces, and nephews—are truly a treasure in my life. None of this would be possible without their support and encouragement. Specifically, I want to mention my older sister Bryna Chinn, who has been a treasured advisor, sharing her wisdom and guidance in all aspects of this journey.

None though is as treasured and impactful in my journey as my wife Naomi. For twenty years Naomi has showered me with the encouragement and nurturing that have made progress possible. I am so incredibly grateful—to you and for you.

Finally, to my dearest friend: Father in heaven, thank You. I love You, and I hope from the bottom of my heart that this makes You proud. I hope that in some way this book expands and expresses the honor of Your kingdom of love and kindness. May it be Your will that this book finds favor in Your eyes and in those who read it—that it might draw You closer to each other in the way it has brought closeness in our relationship.

Foreword

By Rabbi Joey Rosenfeld, LCSW

ONE OF THE universal experiences that unites all of mankind is that we are imperfect. While we all lack differently, the ultimate truth of being human is that we are thrown into the world in a state of deficiency. Whether this lack is perceived as a material deficiency that can be filled with the right amount of financial security, or an emotional deficiency that can be filled with the right amount of attention and affirmation, when all is said and done, human beings experience their own subjectivity through the lens of the lack that rests at the heart of subjectivity. The distinguishing factor between individuals is not whether or not we lack, but rather how we approach our own particular lack. For many, the lack serves as a propelling motivation, incessantly demanding forward motion in hope of discovering the promise of fullness that lies just beyond our reach. The fact that any sense of fullness or perfection that the human being grasps is only momentary, reverting to a newfound sense of deficiency almost as quickly as breath, is one of the more difficult realities of being human. We strive forward in the hopes that our lack will be filled by some object that stands outside of us, only to find that in filling the void, a new type of lack emerges.

The problem with lack is that we are all rooted in a worldview that sees lack as a problem. The world, we are told, was already perfect at the time of Creation, and as such, it was our job as the conscious inhabiters of the world to attune ourselves to the already-present perfection that we found ourselves in. The grand narrative of our beginning that so many of us have incorporated into our psyches—consciously or unconsciously—goes something like this: original man and original woman were placed within a space of fullness—the Garden of Eden. In that space, we are told, we lacked nothing, and everything that the human mind could possibly fathom was present at hand. On the physical level, we were nourished in ways far beyond the mind's comprehension, but what remained clear was that there was no hunger, no thirst, and certainly no craving. On the spiritual level, we were complete, wholly attached to that which we needed. The only thing missing was the sense that something was missing. But, alas, along came the serpent, that primordial source of negativity, and somehow, someway, it locked itself into the human mind. As a result, original man and original woman *sinned*, thereby casting themselves out of their prelapsarian perfection, sullying the natural perfection of the world and damning themselves and their future progeny to a life of suffering and darkness.

The problem with this narrative—beyond the fact that it is simply not true—is that it places human beings within the darkened space of feeling at fault regarding our most basic human condition, namely our imperfection. We were once perfect, and now as a result of our own *sinful* behavior, we have lost our original perfection. The natural outgrowth of such a faulty conception of self is the sense that if only we work hard enough, devour enough, control enough, swallow enough, drink enough, eat enough, use enough, spend enough, we will gain reentry into the Garden, regain our lost perfection, and finally taste the sense of completion we so desperately seek. While this narrative remains deceivingly close to the external truth, it lacks one particular element whose absence has determined that the journey of original man and woman—and by extension, each and every one of us—out of Eden be one of unnecessary suffering.

The element that is missing is lack. If we want to rectify the faulty vision of human subjectivity as falling from perfection, we must first reorient ourselves to our beginning. As the narrative goes, original man and original woman were initially placed within the Garden of Eden, and yes, this Edenic experience represents all that is good and calm and light about the world. We were fed and we were clothed; we knew not of death nor of jealousy. We felt the closeness and connectivity to our particular roles, and most importantly, we lived with a deep awareness of personal meaning. What we were not, however, was perfect. Original man and original woman were placed in the Garden to "cultivate and guard it."[1] The concept of "cultivation" already implies a lack of proficiency, just as the concept of "guarding" implies the susceptibility to failure. The fact that we needed to be warned already implies that we were susceptible to failure. To be susceptible to failure means to be imperfect. To be imperfect means that we are lacking in one way or another, and to be lacking means to be human. This lack, however, is very different than the lack we are used to discussing. It is not some symptom of a fall, nor a sign of not being good enough, but rather it is the very fabric through which we, as creatures, come into this world. The fact that we are inherently imperfect is not an accident—it is constitutive of our very humanity.

In a world that is increasingly cut through with an existential sense of scarcity, it is no wonder that human beings

---

1   Genesis 2:15.

have turned once again to the idols of artificial fullness. Whether it be the undying drive of consumerism that promises satisfaction if just the right amount of money is spent, or the intensification of the drive toward productivity that tells us that if we were only able to produce more we would finally find happiness, the overwhelming mood that seems to cover the earth is that the secret of fullness is out there and it is our fault that we have not discovered it. When we live our lives in the shadow of the false narrative of our beginning, the burdensome brokenness that we carry feels like the direct result of some personal failure. *If only* I were good enough, *if only* I try hard enough, *if only* I forced myself to feel better than I feel. Because the pain of the lack is so strong, we are often willing to grab hold of anything or anyone that will momentarily relieve us from the pain of our imperfection. It is this perspective that so often leads the individual down the path of dependency. If the lack I feel is a momentary deviation from the perfection I am meant to feel, then the quickest route toward filling the lack, which carries the promise of alleviating the pain, becomes the correct route. The undying sense of a desire for some fantastical wholeness that rests just outside my reach quickly transforms into an unbearable craving for some magical *substance*.

One area where this nearly pathological craving for perfection comes into play is the phenomenon of addiction. For those who live with a heightened sensitivity to the lack that cuts through everything in life, any *substance* that provides an artificial sense of *substantiality* quickly moves from the realm of desire to the realm of need and dependency. And even more, with the faulty narrative that teaches us that we are responsible for our lack, we feel as if we must also carry the burden of shame for our imperfection. For if someone has lived their lives with the pervading sense of missing something intangible, and they discover some *substance* or object that brings an immediate sense of wholeness, what is the rational thing to do? Obviously to keep using whatever it is that has brought the newfound fullness into one's life. If a person has been struggling their entire lives to reach the fabled land of perfection, and they taste it in an artificial way through *substance*, they will fight the rest of their lives to recapture that fleeting sense of being whole.

While the issues briefly described above are far more encompassing than any one particular cause, there can be no hope of discovering the origin of suffering without paying close attention to the spiritual blemishes that rest at the core of the issue. If we want to find ways of combating the ever-growing space of addiction in all of its facets, we must learn to understand the *question* that addiction is coming to answer. If the answer that addiction provides is the sense of momentary wholeness and perfection, then the question that animates the addictive quest is this: Where does this undying desire for perfection come from? Where does the need for wholeness emerge? Why do we feel as if imperfection is failure? And most importantly, how can we find comfort within the very thing that makes us human, namely, our experience of lack and imperfection?

Therefore, I feel that Menachem Poznanski's book, *Consciously*, could not arrive at a better moment. In a time that is cut through with an ever-growing awareness of the brokenness of things, in a time where broken souls of chaos are seeking artificial forms of wholeness in every shape of size, *Consciously* introduces us to the possibility of wholeness within the very experience of lack itself. Steeped in the ancient path of Jewish spirituality, as well as contemporary psychological theory, *Consciously* introduces the anciently new idea that with all our imperfections and lack, we hold within ourselves an inherent value that contains everything we need. Contrary to the typical models of psycho-spiritual well-being that promote health by commanding the spiritual seeker out and beyond themselves in order to find the fabled land of perfection that exists beyond them, *Consciously* calmly and lovingly guides the seeker on a path inward where the depths of wholeness have always existed within the constitutive lack that forms human subjectivity. No longer anxious and pressured to fill the void with a perfection that rests just outside of reach, *Consciously* beckons the reader to embrace the "wholeness of limitation" that reminds us that we already have what we need.

Introduction

[T]he spiritual work of a beinoni [a regular person who has achieved spiritual mastery over his life] is…to govern and rule his nature…by means of the spiritual light that radiates in the soul. That is to say, to develop mastery in his heart by means of meditation in the mind on the greatness of the eternal, whereby his understanding begets a spirit of knowledge and reverence of G-d…and [at the same time arouses] love of G-d in his heart…with yearning, desire, and longing revealed in his heart, with a spiritual thirst that emerges out of a fiery flame of passion.[1]

---

1 *Tanya*, part I, *Sefer Habeinoni*, ch. 16. *Tanya*, published in 1796 is the seminal work of the Elder Rebbe of Chabad, Rabbi Shnuer Zalman of Liadi (1745–1812). It is a codification of the basic tenets and fundamentals of Chassidus. Chassidus is a movement within Judaism that was established in 1734 by Rabbi Yisrael Baal Shem Tov. It represented a revolution in Jewish religious and spiritual thought, and as part of its mission, focused on bringing a message of joy, hope, and love to the masses, rooted in the ancient ethical and mystical teachings of the Torah.

YEARNING, DESIRE, LONGING, and fiery passion: all this seems pretty exciting, but are these really terms that belong in an honest discussion about our relationship with G-d? We are not Chassidic Masters—can we actually expect to have fiery passion for the divine? What would that even look like? What would I, or my life, look like if this was really possible?

These were the sorts of questions that lay under the surface of my own spiritual journey for a long time. As a young person, and into my adulthood, I desperately wanted what I perceived to be the spiritual satisfaction I saw in others, yet it felt as if it would never happen.

I had always assumed that a better relationship with G-d must require intense and strenuous effort to be different—to be less myself. I assumed that if I were really serious about my relationship with G-d, I would make major changes to my life. If I wanted spirituality "enough," I would spend long hours delving deeply into spiritual sources and texts, radically change my lifestyle, and dedicate tremendous time to spiritual rite and ritual. Then—maybe then—I would be worthy. I would merit the connectedness I desired, and fulfillment of this desire would lead to the spiritual satisfaction I yearned for.

Yet doing all that felt impossible. In the hustle and bustle of life, it isn't always practical (or even healthy) to suddenly and dramatically change one's life. I didn't always have the stamina or focus for intensive study. I had bills to pay, duties at home, and a career to develop and grow. I had a life. While it might have been thrilling to romanticize what a more intimate relationship with G-d might feel like, actually experiencing that intimacy in a sustainable manner seemed out of reach. I was stuck in this position for a long time.

But then I had to ask myself, what did it all mean if my life was missing one of the integral—perhaps the most integral—ingredients to fulfillment and happiness? What if my assumptions about spirituality—and specifically, conscious connectedness to my Creator—were wrong? Maybe a deep and meaningful relationship with my Creator was, in fact, within my reach and accessible from within my regular life—but I just didn't know how to get there?

Then, something changed. My eyes were opened to a new (and old) way of looking at our world. A path was revealed that I had learned about many times but never understood. Through my experience working with individuals in 12-Step recovery programs,[2] and in learning

---

2 "[The] Twelve Steps are a group of principles, spiritual in their nature, which, if practiced as a way of life, can expel the obsession (to drink) and enable the sufferer to become happily and usefully whole." These

the inner path of Torah from teachers and books, I finally began to understand how spirituality could be real. I came to see that a relationship with my Creator—our Creator, the Creator—isn't fantasy. Indeed, it is the most real thing there is.

One of the most novel aspects of the 12-Step programs is the terminology used to describe spiritual concepts, and one of the most impactful terms for me has been "conscious contact." The term conscious contact describes an intimate, experiential relationship with our Creator, a vibrant connection that is present and guiding. In the first ten steps, the practitioner of the 12-Step program is taken on a journey of self-reflection and spiritual healing, and then guided to an ongoing practice of mindfulness and personal inventory. Then it states in the eleventh step, as a follow-up to this growth: "Sought through prayer and

---

are the words of Bill Wilson (1895–1971), cofounder of Alcoholics Anonymous (AA) and the primary author of the 12 Steps and the *Big Book of AA*. As Aryeh Buchsbayew and I detailed in our book, *Stepping Out of the Abyss: A Jewish Guide to the 12 Steps* (Mosaica Press, 2017), the 12 Steps are a spiritual method and program of recovery that has been adapted hundreds of times to help millions of people gain mastery and recovery from all sorts of addictions and life problems. See this and many other works for a more thorough discussion of the 12 Steps and how they integrate with the Inner Torah philosophy of Judaism.

meditation to improve our conscious contact with G-d, as we understood him…"

I often wondered how exactly that works. Conscious contact seemed to accurately describe what is known in Hebrew as *deveikus*, which was the very thing I had been looking for on my journey. But how exactly would I utilize prayer and meditation to develop a practical conscious relationship with our Creator? Were there practical and down-to-earth directions from within the ancient tradition of my people that would help me to experience this? Where exactly could I find them?

A SPIRITUALLY WHOLESOME LIFE

A spiritually wholesome life is founded upon connectedness to the [Creator]; this is what King David meant when he said, "And for me, closeness to G-d, that is 'good,'"[3] for this is the only good; all that people perceive as good aside from this is only superficiality and illusion.[4]

These are the words of the great Jewish mystic and ethicist, Rabbi Moshe Chaim Luzzatto (the *Ramchal*,

---

3   Psalms 73:28.
4   *Mesilas Yesharim* (the fundamental work of Jewish ethics by Rabbi Moshe Chaim Luzzatto) ch. 1, as quoted in *Bilvavi Mishkan Evneh*, part I, sect. 7.

1707–1746). He invites the reader to view goodness in all things as "good" to the degree and extent to which it allows the individual to develop and experience a relationship with our Creator. Indeed, he sees encountering true good (a vibrant connection with our Creator) as the very purpose of life. To restate it plainly, according to the *Ramchal*: **A healthy connection with our Creator is not only a critical ingredient to fulfillment and happiness but also *the* critical ingredient to fulfilling our very purpose and mission in this world—the "why" of our existence.**

If developing a real connection with G-d is indeed the key to our happiness and the very purpose of our existence, there must be some plan or instruction on how to get there—how to develop a conscious connection. As we will discuss, while from a Jewish perspective, the 613 commandments of the Torah are a pathway to fostering the presence of divinity in our lives, practically, that doesn't always play out as a felt and lived spiritual reality. Many people yearning for connection to the divine make an earnest effort to act out their convictions, yet they are left feeling that their lives are still spiritually barren. A practical and simple step-by-step approach that demonstrates how to utilize and harness the positive spiritual activities already present in our lives is often needed to gain the spiritual fulfillment we are looking for.

In the pages ahead we have sought to do just that—to present a simple action plan, derived from the ancient wisdom of the Inner Torah philosophy,[5] which can help us develop the conscious connection with G-d that we desire. Everything in these pages is rooted in millennia of Jewish mysticism and ethics, particularly as they are presented in the *sefer* (text), *Bilvavi Mishkan Evneh*, Part I.[6] People from

---

5   In the coming pages, we will be referencing and describing our understanding of the ancient wisdom of Torah, and the "Inner Torah" philosophy. For those unfamiliar, the term Torah describes the overall life philosophy of Judaism, which religious Jews believe is divinely bestowed and inspired. While it includes all the basic texts of the Five Books of Moses, the Prophets, and the Writings, and all of their commentaries across the centuries, the term also describes the Talmud and all other legal texts of Judaism, as well as the tradition of stories and vignettes passed down in the midrash. In addition to all of this, which is referred to as the Revealed Torah, there is a corpus of Jewish texts that deals with ethics, mysticism, psychology, philosophy, and theology, which is referred to as the "Inner Torah." This includes the literature of Kabbalah, Machshavah, Chassidus, and Mussar, which were all intellectual movements that sought to capture the message of the Inner Torah and how it informs and influences our existential and spiritual selves and our experience of life. The aspect of Torah we will be discussing here will be through the eyes of this Inner Torah perspective.

6   The themes and concepts we present here are primarily based on one specific work of Jewish ethics entitled *Bilvavi Mishkan Evneh*, part I.

all backgrounds experience fantastic growth and transformation when they commit themselves to an organized and structured growth-based approach. We believe that this specific plan can help anyone, from any background, achieve and/or enhance an experiential connection and relationship with our Creator.

We might assume that ancient religious wisdom that promotes the development of a relationship with G-d would insist that we become more ritualistically observant. Interestingly, this is not the case in the normative sense of those terms. As we will learn, the ancient wisdom

---

Bilvavi Mishkan Evneh (a Hebrew term that translates as "In my heart I will build a Sanctuary") was published anonymously in the early 2000s. The author culled together the teachings of two millennia of ancient wisdom of Torah, describing how we can develop a sustained and healthy conscious relationship with G-d. The author, Rav Itamar Schwartz, has since gained fame in Israel and all over the world as a spiritual teacher and leader to thousands. Aside from some of the exercises, anything that is not sourced directly is an adaptation of that text, and any errors are our own. Our understanding of these concepts, and many of the exercises proposed, were also directly influenced by *Tanya* (in particular, *Sefer Shel Beinonim*, chapters 41 and 42), the teachings of Rebbe Nachman of Breslov (in particular, the sixth Torah in *Likutei Moharan*), and the Lubavitcher Rebbe, Rebbe Menachem Mendel Schneerson (in particular, his Chassidic discourse from 1953 entitled *"Lo Sihiyeh Mishakela"*). Our understanding of *Bilvavi Mishkan Evneh* is also directly influenced by the classes of HaRav Moshe Weinberger, *shlita*, on that *sefer*.

of Torah teaches us to think in the inverse: instead of trying to behave more religiously in an effort to become worthy of a relationship with G-d, we can focus our effort on integrating a relationship with G-d into our lives (which is, no doubt, itself a spiritual and religious "act"), just as we are right now. Then, any behavioral transformation that may occur over time, out of inspiration and conviction, will be the natural and gentle outgrowth of our personal conviction.[7]

Keep in mind, this book is not the work of a guru. It contains neither the guarantee of spiritual ecstasy that will suddenly appear if only you try a little harder, nor the elusive promise of some faraway fantasy of spiritual growth. It doesn't even represent a secret map to an ultimate peak of spiritual achievement. In fact, the approach we will learn together is quite the opposite. It is only a beginning. It is the outgrowth of the experience of spiritual seekers yearning to encounter the most fundamental relationship

---

[7] In modern times, The 12-Step programs have harnessed this type of spiritual approach to the benefit of millions. This attitude stands at the root of the "G-d, as we understood him" concept of the 12 Steps. It teaches that instead of focusing on the faith or G-d-awareness that we don't have, we can start our spiritual journey from where we are right now and grow from there; the faith and awareness we have at this moment are enough to "make a beginning."

10 *Consciously*

of all, the missing ingredient and glue to all our spiritual and material lives: a relationship with our Creator. It is the experience and message of regular people, who live regular lives, and have made the effort to take ownership of their own spiritual journey.[8]

---

[8] Dear reader, we are going to talk about G-d and spirituality, and that's a loaded topic. As such, we want to state clearly that this is not a philosophical book that seeks to prove the existence of G-d or the truth of any particular understanding of G-d. Rather, the goal here, as an expression of our understanding of the book *Bilvavi Mishkan Evneh*, is to present a viable action plan for developing conscious connection and a meaningful relationship with G-d/our Creator—Whoever you understand that to be. We also hope to include some new exercises that will speak to the English audience of spiritual seekers.

Nonetheless, we would like to make it clear that it is not our intention at all to prove anything to you. Our goal is to present a viable plan that when activated, will lead to a real change in consciousness and perspective, and enrich your life with the sense that you have a vibrant relationship with G-d/our Creator, Whoever you understand that to be. If you are still reading, we assume that you want a relationship, or at least want to want one, or are open to wanting one. That is all that is needed to proceed. We hope to provide you with a path that will make it possible to bring that aspiration to fruition in a way that enriches your life and pleases the Creator, Who we believe is waiting for you.

We will utilize the term "our Creator" to refer to G-d in this process for two primary reasons: 1. In the ancient wisdom of Torah, G-d is called by many names, each referring to a different way in which divinity expresses itself in reality. In English, too, the name G-d refers to a divine Being that is present in reality in many different ways. Here, we are specifically speaking about developing a relationship with G-d

What's unique about this method? The most novel part of this approach is the order. We often associate the spiritual journey as the effort we make and the travels we take to find G-d, and to earn the right to have connection and relationship. In this approach, we will discover that we can switch the order; that there is nothing to earn in order to begin. There is no entry price to this ride. We establish the rudiments of a relationship, or more accurately, establish the rudiments of the consciousness of the relationship with our Creator that we already have, and then start our spiritual journey from there. In this context, our spiritual journey is not only a path *to* a greater, more vibrant experience of our Creator, but also a journey we take *with* G-d. This is a pleasant and gentle path of concrete spiritual development and growth that can be passed on from one imperfect seeker to another. It is a path that begins and ends and then begins again, and it is a path that takes on new meaning with every new start.

---

as the Creator. 2. People hold various opinions and understandings of what and who G-d is and how that impacts their lives. Yet, whatever the "truth" is about divine intervention and expectation, we are all creations of a living Creator. As such, we believe—and because you are reading this, we assume you too have some hope or belief—that we all deserve a relationship with that Creator. To honor and remain true to those reasons, we will use the term "our Creator" as often as is possible.

In an effort to make the ideas and concepts accessible, we organized them into a step-by-step approach that can be worked on over time. To help make the process of development gentle and incremental, we broke down the concepts into short chapters. This allows us to read and process the concepts methodically. Hopefully, it also takes into account the hustle and bustle of modern-day life, while also reflecting and respecting the nature of strong and sustainable growth. Often, the most practical and sustainable growth is slow and methodical, not fast and intense. Particularly when we seek to develop our consciousness, attitude, and perception of anything (i.e., the development of new neural pathways and habituated cognitive associations), growth is better framed as a sort of evolutionary process. The development of cognitive muscle memory and attitudinal maturation occurs through the repetition of simple and fundamental practices.

The exercises we have suggested reflect this sort of perspective. We added a section at the end of each step describing practical exercises that will help us achieve the progress we are looking for. These exercises can be practiced at any time and in just a few minutes. Our goal is to provide a resource whose practical application can be achieved with just a few minutes a day.

A note to the reader: The perspectives presented here are based on age-old teachings of the Torah. In order to present an inclusive message (one that as many people as possible can identify with and relate to), we will discuss these ideas as "possible perspectives" with which to see ourselves and life (as opposed to presenting them as absolute fixed moral or philosophical truths). Though for myself, in my own convictions, these perspectives are true, the hope and intention here is to try and avoid alienating anyone in any way and to invite those who do not have the same belief to utilize these perspectives as a way of seeing and approaching spirituality as part of their own efforts to grow.

There are various positions one can take in approaching spiritual concepts, ranging from accepting them as simple fact, to viewing them as a frame through which to see things, or anything in between.[9] In our experience, within

---

9   To illustrate an example of this, later on we will touch on the concept that G-d's presence fills all of reality. This is an idea that could be taken in its most literal form as an expression of what reality actually is (as adherents of Chassidism and Kabbalah—the mystical tradition of Judaism—do). Or instead, a person, more rationalistic in their perspective, could take such a teaching only as a proposed way of looking at and engaging their world, with no need for that influencing their opinion on what reality is. (For example, an individual might develop the mindfulness that sees their world through the lens of focusing on

the context of seeking a spiritual awakening, it doesn't matter which of these positions one takes. (We invite the reader to practice an open-minded approach to all of this. By "open mind" we mean allowing oneself to relate to the concepts according to one's own current conviction, while accepting that others might take an alternative view that is equally legitimate within a process of growth. One will then be open to a change of mind or heart, or the development of new perspectives, by which we mean development and growth according to and within one's own personal convictions.)

As far as the question of who and/or what G-d is or isn't, we have written this book from the position that assumes the reader has some sense that there is a creative divine force with influence over their lives. While my personal beliefs about who and what G-d is and is not are rooted in the teachings of the Revealed and Inner Torah, I believe the messages here are applicable to anyone with a basic faith in a higher force and Creator. For those readers who are

---

the overall influence of a loving higher force and Creator in all things and to look for the impact and influence of that creative force as it manifests and unfolds in his or her life individually, without needing to view that influence as direct, specific, personal or immediate.) This second outlook can be just as meaningful and enlightening, and can just as easily facilitate the sort of growth process we will discuss.

unsure about whether there is a G-d, we would say, "Stick around." If the spiritual path has taught me anything, it is that practical faith is more of an experience than a "thing." Sticking around and trying these exercises might open a door that will allow you to develop convictions about our Creator and about faith you hadn't anticipated. Whatever your experience, we encourage you to continue to pursue your convictions in your own spiritual journey.

Lastly, this book was in many ways written with those in mind who have come to a crossroads in their spiritual process. Talking about G-d is a loaded topic and often brings up a lot of things for many people. As we will touch on much later, coming to terms with our Creator's presence and influence in our lives begs questions and reflections on the meaning behind our own suffering and that which we see all around us. If, as a reader, you find yourself struggling with this sort of thing, don't be surprised: it's a natural part of the process, and you may benefit from seeking out additional support and guidance in addressing those questions as you progress in your relationship with G-d.

An important principle to consider: **A relationship with G-d might be the most therapeutic thing in the world, but it is not a replacement for therapy.**

Many people make the mistake of confusing the therapeutic nature of spirituality for addressing emotional problems, and the outcome can be destructive and disheartening. So we encourage the reader to seek out guidance and help when needed.

With that introduction in mind, we invite the reader to join us on this adventure. We will discover that a vibrant relationship with our Creator is well within our reach, that all the ingredients we need in order to experience the relationship we crave with G-d are right in front of us. Our Creator is not hiding. He can actually be "found" (experienced) in the last place most of us would have thought to look: within our own hearts.

step one

PRIMARY SPIRITUAL PURPOSE

CHAPTER 1

The Importance of Knowing One's Purpose

THE ANCIENT WISDOM of Torah teaches that the success of any process lies in the clear awareness of its goal. In any process, it is critical to understand to the best of our ability where we are going and why we are going there, and to have real hope that we can get there. Then, along the way, as we inevitably encounter challenges,[1] it will be easier to strengthen and bolster our spiritual awareness.

In Hebrew, the term for both "world" and "existence" is *olam*. Exploring the etymology of the word, we find its root is shared with the term for "confusion" (*he'elem*). This symbolism teaches us that our reality naturally breeds a measure of confusion, and that there are inherent paradoxes and anomalies in life that must be traversed when taking the spiritual path. A few examples:

---

1 This doesn't just mean painful or troubling challenges. It can even mean overcoming the challenge of lethargy that comes with success.

- It often seems like nice guys finish last, yet truth consistently wins out in the end.
- Growth is all about action, yet attitude is the key to success.
- To gain mastery and victory over many of life's problems, we must first surrender and admit defeat.
- We turn over our lives to G-d by taking responsibility for our part.

The above paradoxes and others like them, coupled with the hustle and bustle of life, breed a sort of spiritual confusion that often diverts us from our path. This fact is part and parcel of the human experience of life. We all too easily lose clarity on what exactly we are here for.

As we begin the process of developing a vibrant G-d-consciousness, ancient wisdom encourages us to be cognizant of the threat of distortion and confusion that inherently lies ahead. Even after we develop a strong awareness of our spiritual goals, we will need to make a consistent and concerted effort to strengthen our focus on them. Without intervention, we will face the feeling of being lost, confused, and sometimes in despair along the way. Naturally, over time, we may lose perspective of our mission, direction, and destination. To give us the best chance of success, we must therefore develop an action plan of skills to counteract this effect.

So, we will begin our journey by developing a strong understanding of what it is we are trying to accomplish, what spiritual tools we will need, and how we will use them. Through practice, we will begin to develop a sustainable clarity and motivation for what we are doing and why we are doing it. The first concept to take in is to keep in mind that our world exists in such a way that our clarity is challenged at every juncture. It's not a matter of fault or of caring enough or of being serious enough. Rather, we must develop an acceptance of what is; acceptance of a challenge that emerges from the natural order of things. Then, from that place of acceptance, as well as diligence, we can safeguard our mindfulness, adjusting the sails as need be.

CHAPTER 2

Missing the Forest for All the Trees

PLANNING SPIRITUAL GROWTH can be challenging. Simply the idea of attempting to live life differently and more effectively entails taking action and doing "stuff." More often than not, in any effort of change, after the initial burst of excitement, methodically developing ourselves can feel tedious. This dynamic plays out in a new diet, a new commitment to the gym, and many similar efforts to grow. We may not like the current outcome of our way of life, but real change seems like a lot of work.

How can we overcome this natural barrier, and the emotional resistance that is sure to come up, as we start to come to terms with the growth we want?

A famous slogan states: "Don't miss the forest for all the trees." One of the messages behind this proverb perfectly describes the issue at hand. Spiritual practice and growth often seem filled with instructions, actions, and new responsibilities, i.e., the trees that make up the forest. Despite this, we have to keep in our mind's eye the forest itself—the aim of all the meaningful actions we are to take. Our mission here in this approach is developing closeness and attachment to our Creator. We will therefore utilize meditative and expressive exercises to develop a more consistent mindfulness of our mission. This will help generate an internal investment in the process, which will grant us alacrity and excitement, allowing for the necessary effort to grow. Then, as we move on, and when our motivation falters, we will more easily harness resilience to keep going forward. To state it plainly: as we learn to shift our focus from the darkness of the specific to the beauty of the overall journey, the process can become energized and pleasant.

Let us illustrate. If we were lost in a forest (i.e., the darkness of a problem or detail-oriented perspective), all we would see is the individual trees (i.e., all the things that need to be fixed, and all the things we need to do). We would find ourselves in a dark, complicated, and scary existence. But then, if we suddenly went up in a helicopter, our perspective on the forest might shift. We would see a lush panorama of life and color. We would see the size and scope of this beautiful thing called "forest." We would gain a vision of the journey ahead.

Later, when we went back down to the ground, as the darkness would once again creep up on us and our energized passion for the journey would inevitably begin to fade, we could return our mind's eye to the beauty of the whole. The darkness and overwhelming nature of the situation would subside, and our willingness and drive to keep going would return. We could easily remind ourselves that what before seemed overwhelming was not really such a big a deal; that the darkness has an end, and that what made it seem dark is actually beautiful. Freed from the grips of anxiety, hopelessness, or despair, our journey can be a completely new experience. It may even start to be fun.

This is a key to spiritual growth and to combating our natural resistance to change.

To avoid the pitfall of being lost in the minutiae of a thing, we must develop our ability to consistently re-shift our focus back to the beauty of the whole, toward our meaning and our goals.

Practicing this form of mindfulness frees us from the grips of fatigue, anxiety, and fear.[1] It energizes our steps

---

[1] It is important to note that we mean specifically a freedom from the *grip* of these feelings. Any process of substance will entail some measure of

Missing the Forest for All the Trees   25

toward fulfillment and accomplishment. This principle is a mainstay of any spiritual development.

We are setting out on a journey to understand, and put into practice, a simple yet powerful approach that will facilitate a conscious and experiential relationship with our Creator. It requires a healthy and sustained awareness of the primary purpose of the journey, and a plan for bringing that into our lives.

How many times have we tried to work on something, only to find ourselves, a short time later, off the narrow bridge of spiritual growth?

How many times do we have our attitude and energy in just the right place, and then our motivation slips?

What we have learned in these past two chapters is that one of the main reasons this happens is simply because we are humans, living a human experience in a world of paradox. That means that at certain points we will lose perspective, motivation, and drive. We are trying to develop the perspective that this is OK. It's OK, because that's how it goes. Facing this reality is part of the journey. But, it's also OK because now that we know this, we can take proactive steps to counteract the problem, to safeguard a

---

fatigue, anxiety, and fear. It is our ability to face these challenges, to display and practice resilience, that we are looking to develop.

good attitude, and to inspire motivation and drive. This is the focus of the first part of the approach: to develop tools that can continuously draw our consciousness back to our truth and back to effective thinking.

The process is laid out like a ladder so that we can focus on it one rung at a time. The three preparatory rungs will focus on helping us develop a healthy and vibrant desire and commitment to the process. This will give us strength and energy to follow through with the effort ahead and to face challenges that come up. The first step will be developing our ability to consistently draw our minds back to an awareness of the "forest"—the beauty of the whole—which lies in understanding our purpose and mission, the "why" of what we are doing. With this tool in our belt, we will be able to forge ahead on this journey despite any challenges that come up. We begin the process by searching for a deeper understanding of our *primary spiritual purpose*: the primary mission of this process and perhaps life itself.

CHAPTER 3

Individual Mission and Fundamental Mission

WE STARTED OFF by framing the first phase of this process as identifying the primary spiritual purpose. However, before we can accurately identify our spiritual purpose,[1] we will need to first clarify what exactly we are

---

1   It is important to note here that the context of the perspective we are discussing in this chapter has relevance to the individual conviction and life philosophy of the reader. We will be discussing the missionhood of our spiritual lives. For those coming from a religious perspective (specifically, but not exclusively, a classical Torah perspective), our spiritual life and mission, and our general life and mission, is one and the same. In this perspective, even efforts made to develop our material life are fundamentally spiritual acts because they facilitate what is ultimately the purpose of life: a relationship with G-d as expressed when we are channels of the fulfillment of our Creator's vision. From this viewpoint, our underlying spiritual mission is also identifying the underlying purpose of life itself. The same could be said for someone coming from a 12-Step perspective, where the intended result of the practice of the steps is spiritual awakening and living a life of service as a channel of one's G-d or higher power. In this framework, all aspects of life become a space in which to practice principles and carry a

looking for. What does "primary purpose" mean in the context of our spiritual lives? A wonderful frame that helps illustrate this point is to look at the difference between an *individual mission* and a *fundamental mission* in life.[2]

The ancient wisdom of Torah teaches that the areas that puzzle us most, and which we struggle with most, are the very areas in which our individual purpose and missions lie.[3] An example of this is when an addict or alcoholic realizes that they wield a powerful weapon over their illness and have the opportunity to flood their life with tremendous meaningfulness by being useful to a fellow sufferer—that, as a recovered or recovering alcoholic and/or addict, they have a special mission to help other alcoholics and addicts. In other words, their

---

message. Nonetheless, if you are coming from a different perspective, one that recognizes a separation between the development of one's "spiritual" life and one's general purpose in life, the association of the content in this chapter will be slightly different. In that case, we invite the reader to see this as a discussion about the purpose and mission of our spiritual efforts to effect a relationship with our Creator, and not as the underlying purpose of life itself.

2   As we will see ahead, the term "fundamental mission" is not a reference to a global, communal, or cultural mission of a number of people. Rather, the concept here is that within our own personal mission, there is both an individual/subjective mission and a fundamental/objective mission.

3   As quoted in *Bilvavi Mishkan Evneh*, part I, sect. 4.

Individual Mission and Fundamental Mission 29

greatest "weakness" can become—and in a sense, already is—one of their most meaningful strengths. This sort of meaningfulness takes place in nearly every area of major life challenge. Often, people find the resilience to face and overcome their struggles through understanding that by overcoming them, they will represent a beacon of hope for those still struggling similarly. Many times, this plays out when people overcome an illness, the loss of a loved one, or a certain disability. It is quite common that helping others who are going through this very struggle becomes a driving force in their lives. Their lives become infused with a deep sense of meaning and purpose, which helps them to carry on in facing their own struggles, while simultaneously utilizing their experiences in the service of others.

Now, if we walked down the street and interviewed different growing and spiritually minded people, asking about their individual mission and purpose (i.e., what they are currently dedicated to working on), each might give a different answer:

- "I struggle with anger and I need to work on my self-control when I get upset."
- "I gossip too much; I'm not careful enough with my speech."
- "I need to work on my relationship with my spouse."

If we fast-forwarded a couple of years and asked these same people what happened when they finally achieved success, they may likely point to some project that emerged in their lives, related to these areas, which has given them a great sense of purposefulness. An anger-management support group, a WhatsApp group for people working on speaking properly that posts daily inspiration, an initiative to strengthen marriages, or simply having had the opportunity to share their strength and hope with someone else who just happened to mention they were struggling with the same problem—all this is inspiring, amazing, and wonderful.

Now, all of these are obviously meaningful areas for a person to work on and develop, and they represent individual missions for each of these people. But if they were to stop there in their spiritual development—at their individual mission—they would be missing out. The ancient wisdom of Torah teaches us that underlying our individual life mission is a fundamental mission that every person in the world shares. Surprisingly, this perspective actually teaches that the answer to the riddle of why we feel spiritually malcontent is not to be found by looking at what we particularly struggle with (although that is absolutely necessary for growth and adds great fulfillment to our lives), but rather because we need to look more keenly at the mission that every person in this world shares with us: the objective, overall mission of our spiritual journey.

The ancient wisdom of Torah reveals that the fundamental mission of our lives is actually the ingredient we've been searching for to bring our otherwise fractured inner life together. Embracing this mission acts as the glue for our spiritual journey. Therefore, to have the success we want, in addition to working on our personal and individual shortcomings, we will need to focus time and attention on our spiritual development.

Often, people take the underlying fundamental mission for granted and consequently lose sight of where they are going in life, why they are headed there, and how they intend to make it. We pointed out previously how counterproductive this can be. Our first step here toward improving our spiritual health, and developing conscious contact specifically, is not to be found in our unique and personal struggles, but rather in an area of need we share with everyone around us. Clarifying this area of need—and therefore, our fundamental mission—will usher in a spiritual stability that will act as the foundation of a meaningful relationship with our Creator. It is what we call—and how we will define—our primary spiritual purpose. Our primary spiritual purpose is the underlying mission which everyone around us is also charged with. We now need to further clarify what this underlying, fundamental mission actually is.

CHAPTER 4

What Is Our Primary Spiritual Purpose?

NOW THAT WE have explained the importance of having a clarity of mission and explained which mission we are specifically referring to—the underlying fundamental mission common to all of us—it is time to try and develop an answer and perspective on what our primary spiritual purpose is.

If we were to survey some ardently religious people about this question, we might assume their answer to be: "Our fundamental mission is to serve G-d by adhering to His laws and carrying out whatever He demands." Ancient Torah wisdom teaches that this is actually an understatement and in some ways an oversight; like all spiritual disciplines, the devil is in the details. While positive spiritual acts and study of religious texts are absolutely integral to serving G-d within a religious context, we need to always remember that they are means to an end.[1] So the question we will seek to answer is, what are the ends we are seeking?

The ancient wisdom of Torah teaches (as discussed in many sources and expressed explicitly in the words of the *Ramchal*) the ends that G-d prescribes for us: the primary spiritual purpose of our lives is *sheleimut*, meaning, "a spiritually wholesome life."

Let's explore what this means.

None of us aspire to be a broken person or to have a broken life. Just as we aim at all costs to avoid brokenness in many facets of our lives—physical, material, emotional, as well as in relationships—we also don't want to settle for spiritual brokenness. Indeed, we are aiming for a spiritually wholesome life.

---

[1] As it relates to Judaism specifically, this perspective is well supported by the known and often-quoted statement of the *Zohar*, the ancient mystical text that teaches that the *Taryag Mitzvot*, the 613 Commandments of Torah, are actually *Taryag Itim*, 613 suggestions or directions of how a Jew establishes and maintains a relationship with their Creator. In the spiritual and inner-world perspective, the ultimate motive of a religious life is not religious behavior, because action and behavior are but a means to an end. The ultimate motive is the relationship itself. In this context, religion is less an institution and more a program for developing attachment and connection to our Creator.

What Is Our Primary Spiritual Purpose? 35

What, though, is "a spiritually wholesome life"? Is spirituality ever really complete? How can we define the completeness of one's spirituality?

The first answer that might come to mind is perfection. That in order to be complete, we will need to be perfect. Yet, is this what G-d expects from us? Can it be true that our goal is perfection and anything that falls short of this is failure and brokenness? If this were true, we would all be in deep trouble, as we are all flawed and have many shortcomings.

As we highlighted in the introduction, from the perspective of the ancient wisdom of Torah as taught by the *Ramchal*,[2] a spiritually wholesome life is defined by a deep and meaningful connectedness to G-d. In this perspective, the completeness of our spiritual life is not measured by the degree of our own perfection, but rather by the degree to which the light of the divine is manifest and expressed in our lives.

Where does this concept come from? From where does the *Ramchal* draw this idea?

It comes from none other than perhaps the greatest ethicist, poet, and philosopher of all time: the Psalmist

---

[2] As taught explicitly by the *Ramchal* in *Mesilas Yesharim*, chap. 1 (see Introduction to this work for more detail), as quoted in *Bilvavi Mishkan Evneh*, part I.

King David, when he says, "For me, closeness to G-d, that is 'good'" (Psalms 73:28). If we take this statement of David literally, as the *Ramchal* suggests, King David is telling us that closeness to G-d is the essence of goodness, the essence of life. The implication here is that the extent to which a particular situation or thing brings us to an experience—and/or a channel—of G-d, is the extent to which that thing is good, i.e., wholesome or complete.

Let's unpack that, though. Are we proposing that there is no other goodness in the whole world? Anyone who has experienced this world knows there is much to enjoy. Ice-cream tastes great and steak is delicious, but they don't seem particularly connected to getting close to G-d! What then does this mean?

To further explain, let us rephrase what the *Ramchal* is suggesting. While there is much goodness in this world, this spiritual approach proposes that my ability to experience the full extent of goodness within anything is in direct proportion to how that person, place, thing, or situation reflects and honors my connection to our Creator. Seen through this lens, the goodness of this world is not good in and of itself, but rather "goodness" is the means by which each thing reflects the ultimate aim of the universe—a felt closeness to G-d.

Now that we have a clearer definition of what the ancient wisdom of the Torah means by a spiritually wholesome life—a sense and state of closeness to G-d—we have a better understanding of this perspective on our primary spiritual purpose. In the eyes of ancient Torah wisdom, as expressed by King David and explicitly interpreted by the *Ramchal*, a person whose life is whole, a person who is not broken, is a person who is connected to G-d. To state this spiritual perspective plainly: **Closeness to G-d is the primary spiritual purpose of our life.**

THE SOUL OF LIFE

A concept in Jewish mysticism states that just as all created things have a soul and a body, so too, concepts and themes have a soul aspect and a bodily aspect. If we reflect on how this relates to our topic, the mission of our lives would be the soul, while the content of our lives would be the body. Just as a body that is devoid of a soul is dead, so too, a life without fulfillment of our fundamental mission—without attachment to G-d—is a "dead" life.

An ancient Jewish teaching states: "A *rasha* (wicked person) is called dead during his lifetime."[3] If we reflect

---

3   *Berachos* 18b.

further on this and try to approach it from a positive and practical spiritual perspective (rooted in the teachings of Chassidus and Kabbalah), we might understand this teaching as follows: A *rasha* (one whose life is completely dominated by their base instincts) is called dead, not because they are actually dead; rather, because they are one whose life is disconnected from its true purpose. They have become completely enslaved to whatever they feel or want and therefore cannot be dedicated to what they believe in or have conviction toward. They are constantly overwhelmed by distracting impulses and are thereby removed from living their life as a journey toward wholesome completeness. Their life has a body but is missing its soul.

We have proposed that the fundamental mission of our spiritual lives is the opportunity to grow in closeness to our Creator. If we accept that as a truth, then the moments we are aware of and experience this closeness are the moments in which we are truly alive.

As mentioned, there are stumbling blocks to keep in mind as we take this journey:

- The nature of the world is such that it breeds confusion; the spiritual journey is one of seeming spiritual paradoxes.

- The nature of spiritual growth is to first appear complex and overly demanding. Complexity blocks out the beauty of the whole, and can feel dark and overwhelming.
- On our spiritual journey, we often get caught up in or overwhelmed by the means and lose sight of the end.

We discussed how critical it is that we rise above the gloominess of the details and the particularities of the journey, to recognize unity within and without. We reflected on the purpose of the details of our lives, the purpose we share with all people—the underlying spiritual purpose, perhaps, of life itself. Then we proposed that tapping into this unifying perspective is the key we've been missing in our spiritual journey.

STEP 1: PRIMARY SPIRITUAL PURPOSE—KNOW YOUR PURPOSE

In Step 1, we began the preparatory stages of the process of spiritual growth. These initial steps are universal in nature and can be applied to almost any effort to develop and grow. In Step 1, we were seeking to gain clarity of our purpose, not just the purpose of this effort, but rather the primary purpose of our whole spiritual life.

Continued recognition of our primary spiritual purpose is the integral ingredient of our spiritual success, serenity, and contentment.

We moved ahead by working to keep our mind's eye keenly focused on the forest and not the trees. We aimed to see the whole—the mission we share with everyone—and to look at our journey through the lens of spiritual unity, while maintaining our focus on the purpose of what we are working for. This clarity, the clear recognition within our innermost self of our primary spiritual purpose, is the work of Step 1.

We have proposed a clear vision and perspective on what the primary spiritual purpose is, but we invite the reader to search within their own conviction. The main thrust of Step 1 was that we must have clarity in our spiritual efforts. We must accept and understand that the pursuit of spiritual development and a relationship with G-d is not some empty impulse. It is the fulfillment of something we hold sacred and dear, something we believe in. It is only with such conviction that we will be able to face the challenges ahead and stay the course of living true to ourselves and our spiritual convictions. The work of Step 1 entailed asking ourselves: What is my primary and fundamental spiritual purpose? What are we are all doing here, in relation to the spiritual aspects of our lives?

The ancient wisdom of Torah says that our primary purpose is this very thing: conscious contact, a relationship with G-d. If we accept that simple premise, then by reading on and carrying out the exercises in this book, we will be doing more than just a "nice thing." We will be making the earnest attempt to move toward the fulfillment of the spiritual purpose of life itself.

What an exciting thought, what a beautiful journey to undertake!

Into Action—Step 1: Primary Spiritual Purpose

DOWN IN BLACK AND WHITE

Practice: Write It Down

If we ran into the world's foremost expert on commodities and investments (or any field we desperately wanted and needed to know about), and he or she wanted to share with us the secret to their success and fortune, we would no doubt immediately take out a piece of paper and write it down. We would do this for two reasons:

1. Writing the information would help it become more concretely established in our minds.
2. We wouldn't want to forget what we'd been told. If at any point we lost awareness, we could look back at our notes and right our ship.

Surprisingly, the most important element of spirituality is its stability. When spirituality lacks stability, it lacks sustainability. Stability is created and sustained through simple steps, like writing down our understanding of the purpose of one's spiritual life on a small piece of paper and carrying it with us at all times. Having this note available and reading it at various times throughout the day can ensure clarity on our spiritual journey.

The goal in this process is *not* to build an intense yet unstable relationship with our Creator. As is the case in any relationship, creating a place in our hearts for our Creator that crumbles under the weight of life lacks a certain measure of meaning. If we are developing a real relationship, we want one that will be there when we need it most, and one we can show up for when times are toughest. We are seeking a path toward a relationship with G-d that is strong and sturdy, one that can survive and even thrive through the ups and downs that life throws at us.

We can start the process of laying a spiritual foundation of resilience by doing just the sort of simple action we described above. As we gain deeper clarity of the fundamental mission of our spiritual lives, we can write it down on a piece of paper and carry it in our pocket wherever we go, being mindful to keep it close. We can then take it out throughout the day and remind ourselves why we are doing what we are doing and affirm to ourselves that what we are doing will bring us closer to the "why" of our spiritual lives. The fundamental tool of simple repetition underlies this concept.

We can begin by taking a small piece of paper and writing on it the primary spiritual purpose of our life. Perhaps start with the words of the Psalmist: "For me, closeness to G-d, that is 'good.'" Or identify, in quick and simple terms, the way in which your current conviction describes the primary spiritual purpose. We can practice this procedure at the beginning of the day, writing this out and placing the note in our pockets, our cellphone cases, or wallet. Then, throughout the day, we can take it out and read it verbally, practicing being mindful that the fundamental spiritual purpose of our lives is connection and attachment with our Creator. Despite the complexity and multilayered nature of life, there is a simple unifying reason behind it all, a soul to our existence. And even though it doesn't always feel that way, we are in an exquisite and majestic forest, and there is an underlying whole to the pieces and details of life. Experience of that whole is the gift of a lived existence (as opposed to the opposite), a life of experienced conscious contact with G-d.

step two

CONSCIOUSNESS OF CONTACT

CHAPTER 5

What Is Closeness to G-d?

HAVING IDENTIFIED "CLOSENESS" to G-d as a possible barometer for having a wholesome and complete life, we now require a more thorough working definition for what that actually means. What does it mean to be close to our Creator? What exactly is the ancient wisdom of Torah encouraging us to do?

Let us start to break this all down by defining closeness as it is used in Hebrew. *Kirvah*, meaning "closeness" or "relatedness" of one person or thing to another, can be divided into two categories:

1. **Spatial closeness**: the physical or material proximity of any two variables
2. **Interpersonal closeness**: the type or level of loving closeness—the intensity and strength of one's feeling and commitment for another person, group, or thing

This leaves us with a significant question. We said that the ancient wisdom of Torah defines our fundamental spiritual mission as closeness to G-d, yet in the most simple context of both spatial and interpersonal closeness, no further effort or action would be necessary by anyone to have a "complete life" because we are already close to G-d. In fact, who is closer to us than our Creator?

Let's illustrate:

The ancient wisdom of Torah teaches that our Creator's influence and presence fills the space of all our reality. If this is the case, then from the perspective of the Torah, we couldn't be any closer spatially to our Creator if we tried. We are technically closer to our Creator than the chair we are sitting on or even the clothes we are wearing. We are spatially closer to G-d than anything else.

We can say the same thing from the perspective of the ancient wisdom of Torah in relation to interpersonal closeness. How do we know that an individual is a relative or friend? Because they say so. For example, we know our father is our father because he (or someone else) tells us that he is, and we have other corroborative evidence to support that; for example, he demonstrates in action that this is true, or we resemble him. As a result, we trust that he is, in fact, our father. This is in spite of the fact that, barring a genetic paternity test, we don't actually *know* it for sure. A similar distinction holds true for friends. How do we know that an individual is our friend? First, because they say they are our friend, and then because they demonstrate in action that this is so.

The Torah is filled with passages that describe our Creator not only as one particular relative, but as many kinds of relatives. The Creator is described as our parent, our best friend, as well as many others. In essence, the Torah invites us to see the Creator as the closest possible relative we have.[1]

Therefore, in the eyes of the ancient wisdom of Torah, what is left for us to do in developing our spirituality? So much for our fears about too much effort! If "a spiritually wholesome life" is defined by our closeness to our Creator, do we fulfill our primary spiritual purpose by simply existing?

This perspective introduces a most pleasant and meaningful paradigm shift: **Seeing as we are already closer to our Creator than anything else, we can conclude that it is not closeness to G-d that we need to strive for—we are granted that precious gift the moment we are born. Our Creator is to be found all around us and within us.**

---

1 *Bilvavi Mishkan Evneh*, part I, sect. 29. The text quotes two specific sources that state this kind of intimate relation with G-d: "You are children to the Lord your G-d…" (Deuteronomy 14:1), and "Do not forsake your Friend and your father's Friend [in context of referencing G-d]…" (Proverbs 27:10).

If that is the case, the "work" ahead will not entail *creating* contact; instead, it will entail *developing* a robust cognizance and mindfulness of the connection that is already there. Plainly put: **Our fundamental purpose in life is to develop a sustained consciousness of the connection with our Creator that we already have.**

We don't need to create something new in order to have a fundamentally successful and meaningful spiritual life.[2] The gift is already here—we were granted that at birth. Our work lies in waking up to the reality of the existing gift. This is what our approach will be focusing on.

---

[2] It is interesting to note that this concept (i.e., of the fulfillment of missionhood not being hinged on growth or change) does not include those areas that are within our individual mission. These almost always require growing and developing ourselves in a way that is not currently present, and require overcoming challenges by learning new skills and maturing ourselves, as well as changing our behavior. What we end up with, then, is a very specific difference between our subjective/individual mission and our fundamental/objective mission. The former requires a deep effort to develop and grow and then to create change in action and thought, while the latter is more about acknowledgment, acceptance, and gratitude for what we have already been given.

CHAPTER 6

Is Wholesome Completeness Really Possible?

WE PROPOSED THAT the primary spiritual purpose of our lives, "a spiritually wholesome life," is having a conscious relationship and connection with our Creator. This is made possible by developing cognizance and mindfulness of the deep connection with G-d that we already have. As we explore this aspiration, we might catch ourselves thinking: "Is this even possible for me? Maybe someone who has the presence of mind to meditate or study spiritual texts for many hours a day can maintain awareness of their connection with their creator, but I'm just a regular person! How can I accomplish this? And even if I do, how can I live a normal life in this way?"

To address these reservations, we first have to identify the common source of such nagging, cynical thoughts. When we make progress in any process of spiritual development, we come in contact with an internal critical voice that seems to always highlight past mistakes and project fear-centered promises of failure. These pessimistic thoughts often stem from a cynical part of ourselves that is resistant to and fearful of change, rather than a healthier and more prudent form of skepticism.

If we have any chance of success, we will have to admit that within us is a force that *seems* to want to divert us from our spiritual aspirations. That part of us will go to any length to convince us that it is impossible for us to succeed and impossible to experience a meaningful relationship with our Creator and to achieve a spiritual life.

Ancient Jewish Wisdom calls this part of us the *yetzer hara*, literally, the "evil inclination." In 12-Step recovery lingo, people sometimes call this "my disease," while in other cultures it is called by different names. The common denominator of all these terms is the acknowledgment of a force within us that is self-sabotaging. These cynical outlooks emerge from fear, anger, and a lack of healthy self-esteem. Though healthy skepticism can be a vital aspect of growth, when it emerges out of a place of negativity, fear, and dysfunction, it is of no use—and is nearly always untrue. There may be some layers of quasi-truth to it, but overall, it is the ranting of an immature, bruised, and hurt part of ourselves, which is terrified of change.

As we progress, we will need to practice identifying these counterproductive voices and develop the awareness that this inner force is not speaking the truth. We need to have the courage to believe that a life of spiritual elevation is, in fact, well within our reach, and will not demand from us more than we can give.

Yet, having acknowledged the roots of cynical and resistant thoughts, how do we now address our earlier questions? Is a wholesome, spiritual life really practical? Is it really possible for us?

The *Ramchal*, whom we quoted earlier, teaches that the deepest and highest levels of spiritual growth and ascension are not reserved for individuals who are perfectly righteous.[1] He teaches that the key ingredient to spiritual elevation is actually a true conviction and commitment to live one's life for the sake of heaven, and that anyone whose life is lived dedicated to the ultimate good (as defined by the will of our Creator—as we understand it) can achieve the deepest levels of spiritual fulfillment and expression. Whether we spend the bulk of our time at work, meditating, or studying religious texts is not what's important per se. The main question is, to what degree are the overall individual actions of our lives in line with our understanding of our Creator's will? If we are living in

---

1   *Mesilas Yesharim*, as quoted and explained in *Bilvavi Mishkan Evneh*, part I, p. 13.

opposition to what we understand to be our Creator's will, and living at odds with the universe, our consciousness of the presence of G-d becomes understandably blotted out. But, when our lives are lived (to the best of our ability) in line with the flow of creation, the Creator is everywhere to be found, especially in our hearts.

At first glance, this might feel overwhelming. "Living my whole life for the sake of heaven? That seems like a lot to ask!"

If we reframe our perspective, though, we can see how reality is quite different.

As an exercise, let's consider how much of our lives are already perfectly in line with how we perceive our Creator wants us to live. Obviously, we each have areas of life where we fall short of our ideals. Yet, these are most likely a few moments in the scope of things. Most of our active life is likely spent engaged in all sorts of positive activity—seeking to connect with others and doing fundamentally good things that our Creator surely wants for us. Whether it's caring for our children, studying in school for a career, attending spiritual gatherings, calling a friend on the phone to catch up and see how they're doing, holding the door for someone, or even sleeping and eating so we have the energy we need to continue and to grow, our lives are surely filled to the brim with meaningful, positive action.

The question therefore is *not* whether we are doing good things—because we surely are. The question, rather, is whether we have the mindfulness to do those good things specifically with the will of our Creator in mind.[2] Of course, as humans, we do things with multilayered intent. Yet, through the use of mindfulness, we can direct our focus and intention to the higher motives of our behavior, instead of letting our baser motivations drive us.

What we are talking about in essence is not necessarily changing our lives. Certainly, in the process of evaluating our motives and developing spiritual motivations, we may decide to be more careful about certain behaviors in some areas, but that is not operative. We are again proposing a paradigm shift: What will make or break our ability to internalize spiritual lessons and transform our lives is a simple change in the way we think—a change in our attitude and perspective. We need to work to create a psychic shift in how we see our lives and our awareness of the *good* things our lives are already full of. We need to shift our

---

2   Instead of, for example, allowing more superficial motivations to completely dominate our deeds, like perhaps acting well because of an instinctual need, or to satisfy other people's expectations or other such motivations. Obviously, all actions have a multiplicity of motivations, and the point here is which motivation is dominant.

focus away from what we may be doing wrong to what we are doing right. We can then invite G-d into those areas.

When we make this simple psychic shift, no longer living in the hamster wheel of self-will (where even good deeds are dominated by self-serving motives) and instead living life according to our understanding of our Creator's will for us, we may change some of our behavior, but our overall life will probably pretty much stay the same.

Let's illustrate:

An individual with a family works at an accounting firm, clocks in eight hours a day at work, plus two hours of travel time. Before he or she leaves in the morning, they may say prayers, spend a few minutes with the children, and perhaps read something interesting and/or inspirational. When he or she gets home, there's dinner with the family, quality time with a spouse, and then maybe a couple times a week going out to play a sport, engage in a hobby, go to a spiritual class or community advocacy meeting (or perhaps a recovery meeting—to hear a nice speaker, share a message of hope, and reach out to new people). Then he or she returns home to pay some bills, make some calls to check in with others and see how they are doing, and relax for a few moments. Our accountant spends the weekends with family and friends, and maybe takes a nice vacation a couple times a year. Though he or she surely makes mistakes, overall, this person lives a wholesome life.

If we posed the question about the viability of living a wholesome and complete spiritual life to our accountant, they might say, "Real conscious contact, that's not for me—I'm just a regular person. Maybe if I was some kind of guru or intensely religious person, I could achieve that, but me? If I'm lucky, I'll get to feel spiritual once in a while..."

The surprising truth, though, is that according to the ancient wisdom of Torah, this is simply not accurate. Our accountant can, in fact, achieve real Conscious Connection in his or her current life, as it is right now.

The question is not whether they worked eight hours a day, or studied, prayed, and meditated eight hours a day. The question is largely about the mindset they have when they get on the train in the morning.

We can develop the attitude and mindful consciousness that it is an incredibly spiritual and meaningful act to work, make a living to support our families, give to others, and nearly all the other things that we are busy with. All we need to do is shift our perspective. We need to say to ourselves something like, "Today, I'm going to go to work as an expression of my Creator's will. My Creator wants my family to have abundance, joy, and security, and I have the opportunity to be an active participant in that process. My Creator wants to give me the opportunity to share my abundance with those who are needy and for them to receive it. My commitment is that I'm not only going to spend time with my children today because it makes me feel good, or because I don't want to feel guilty about it later. Rather, I get to, with the intention that honors the privilege I have of being a parent to my children, which is a gift from my Creator. I am privileged to shower my children with love and affection 'for free and for fun, because I want to,' and because I can. I will be true to the blessing and duty our Creator granted me."

We can repeat this sort of mantra and prayer about every aspect of our lives.

STEP 2: CONSCIOUSNESS OF CONTACT—DEVELOP HOPE FOR SUCCESS

Step 2 in this process was about developing a sense of hope that we can actually achieve the spirituality we are looking for. This began by developing the awareness that from the perspective of the ancient wisdom of Torah, we already have what we've been looking for. The spiritual aspiration of a relationship with our Creator is not something we can "get"—it's something we can wake up to. We began to live a life of conscious contact by simply directing our attention to how much of our life is already for the sake of heaven. Such mindfulness actualizes and honors how close our lives already are to G-d. Through this effort of acknowledging the aspect of our motivation that is dedicated to G-d's will, we can invite our Creator's presence into every crevice of our lives. In doing so, we shower much of our life with spiritual meaning and sanctity. The crux of this effective, sustainable, and fulfilling spiritual way of life is simply this: **We don't need to change anything on the outside to transform the inside. As we stand right now, we have the opportunity to bring the consciousness of the presence of our Creator into real time.**

Into Action—Step 2: Consciousness of Contact

BEING TAPPED IN AND FOR HEAVEN'S SAKE

Practice #1: Being Tapped In

Practice meditating on the contact with the Creator that already exists in your life. Reflect on how close to our Creator we already are, spatially and interpersonally. If you are not used to simple meditative practice,[3] sit quietly in a chair for one minute, timing yourself. After one minute of silence, take some breaths, taking air in through your nose and expelling your breath slowly through your mouth. Count eight total breaths, four in and four out. Just as your breath fills your body, as the oxygen is carried

---

3   The word "meditation" carries a host of associations, and often a connotation that meditation is unreasonable or aloof. While meditation can be a deeply intense practice, that is not the sort of meditation that we are talking about here. All that is needed is simple reflection that does not take more than three to five minutes. If you are new to meditation, you might find it useful to utilize the many resources available that help train a person in the practice of simple meditation. There are video clips online, as well as very easy-to-use phone and tablet apps that can help train a person in this area. Committing to even ten consecutive days of guided meditation can make an enormous difference in a person's ability to incorporate the suggestions and practices recommended in this process.

by your bloodstream to every part of you, experience G-d filling your existence, filling the space of your body and material self. The influence and impact of our Creator is everywhere we turn—closer spatially then the chair you are in and the clothes you are wearing. The Creator's presence is everywhere, inside and out. When this is complete, spend one to five minutes in silence, reflecting on the ideas above, and allowing it all to sink in.

In another meditation exercise, start with breathing as we described above and reflect on the closeness you feel to your closest relatives. Reflect on the concept that you are *more* "related" to our Creator, or related in more ways to our Creator, than anyone else in your life—our Creator is your closest relative.

End the meditation with a prayer, in plain words. Perhaps a prayer of thanks and gratitude for the unique and special relationship you have already with our Creator, and your hope to grow in awareness and appreciation of that relationship.

Practice #2: For Heaven's Sake

Having developed a greater awareness of the closeness to the Creator that is already present in your life, turn your attention to how that closeness is present in your active life. Focus your mind for a few minutes, internalizing how much of your life is already in line with—and an expression of—the goodness G-d wants for you and others. Make a list of all the things you already do that are in line with your perception of the Creator's will and goodness.

Now let's develop an openness to a life of Conscious Connection by focusing in a simple and spiritual way on living for the "sake of heaven." For example, when you take any positive actions in your life, practice the simple thought, which you can even state in prayer out loud: "I am doing this good deed for a greater good, as an expression of the Creator's will for me—as a channel of creative light and a reflection of G-d's presence in all of my life." Or, when you begin your day, take a moment to reflect on all that you hope to do in the day ahead, especially the parts that are obviously good and necessary for a purposeful life. Perhaps say a simple prayer that acknowledges that you are living for the sake of heaven, for the spreading of the Creator's light. Close the prayer with gratitude—for the opportunity to live a spiritual life of service and goodness.

Affirm for yourself that being able to have a life infused with spirituality and lived with our Creator is a gift. A life of conscious contact.

step three

WILLINGNESS TO CONNECT

CHAPTER 7

Do I Actually Want Conscious Contact?

LET'S START WITH a quick review of the perspective we are presenting. We began this process by proposing a framework for identifying our spiritual purpose in life. We separated this into two categories: our personal and our fundamental spiritual missions. The ancient wisdom of Torah teaches the following:

- Our personal spiritual mission relates to areas of struggle or meaning; areas of our lives where our Creator is inviting us to effect growth and change.
- Our fundamental spiritual mission is one all people share, and it focuses on developing closeness to G-d.

We then clarified that although our fundamental spiritual mission is to develop closeness with our Creator, from the perspective of the Torah, we couldn't get closer to G-d if we tried. Our Creator fills our existence, which is spatial closeness, and our Creator is related to us in every possible way, which is interpersonal closeness. Closeness to G-d is something inherent.

How does enhancing our closeness to our Creator manifest as a spiritual practice? It means developing our capacity for a sustained mindfulness of the connection we were granted at birth—developing a consciousness of contact.

We then discussed how developing this mindfulness is possible no matter what our general lifestyle is. The key to achieving an active awareness of the presence of G-d does not lie in living an ascetic life removed from this world, or studying religious and/or spiritual texts all the time, but rather, in accustoming ourselves to consciously live our lives according to the Creator's will. We pointed out that when looking through a spiritual lens, so much of our lives are a reflection of what our Creator wants both for and from us, and we practiced acknowledging the elements of our life that are already in line with G-d's will. By doing so, we began to live our lives for the sake of heaven. With this, we invite a consciousness of our Creator's presence into all the areas of our life.

The bridge we now need to cross is willingness. To move ahead, we must answer honestly the following questions:

- "Do I actually want a spiritual life?"

- "Do I actually want to be meaningfully conscious of my connectedness with my Creator?"
- "Do I want to align my will with His will?"

As we mentioned above, having a meaningful awareness of our Creator's acute presence in our lives doesn't require significant change to one's lifestyle; but as a real and felt consciousness of G-d takes shape in our lives, some measure of change is likely to occur.[1] When our relationship with our Creator is vibrant and present, and we become cognizant of the harmful impact of certain activities on our feelings of connectedness, inspiration to grow or change our behaviors often occurs. Certain ambivalence or cognitive dissonance about certain behaviors may shift. People who earnestly live with a meaningful consciousness of the presence of our Creator (or to reframe, people who live an actually spiritual life) live a certain way.

Do we really want to live that way?

---

[1] Though we have already stated this, it is worthwhile to reiterate that we are not referring to becoming more religiously observant per se, or any other specific changes. We are referring to the natural change that occurs within a person and in their life when their G-d-consciousness is stronger and more meaningful. This kind of change can include religious growth or development, but might also simply entail a shift in perspective on one's practices in relationships or other applications of life.

Are we willing to receive the outcomes and benefits that a spiritual life of conscious contact with our Creator offers?

This is a question that we have to face honestly. We must uncover, discover, and with G-d's help as time goes on, discard, the internal resistances to growth that lie hidden in our hearts. Allowing these feelings to operate beneath the surface will only impede our growth as we move on in the process.

A fairly common mistake people make is skipping over the step of developing willingness. We identify an area of need and associate growth and change as something we don't really have choice about. "Of course I have to change," we think. "Now that I see this as truth, I don't have a choice." But then, when resistance emerges, the only tool available to motivate action is to "try harder." We push ourselves, but eventually, as this pattern repeats, we become mired in the sense that we are only exerting ourselves to act on something we don't actually want. The opportunity for growth has become a burden, something we "have to do." If we haven't done the work to own and develop an earnest desire to grow and face any unwillingness head-on, we end up treating our personal development like an imposition. While it may be true that the alternative to growth or engaging in growth is so untenable that it seems like there is no other choice, that doesn't mean choice—and our own ownership of that choice to grow—is not real.

To counter this effect, we have to step back at certain points and take action to develop the willingness to act on our convictions. We need to remind ourselves of what we want to do and identify the feelings of resistance that come up. We need to make clear that they are not us, but rather, as we mentioned earlier, these "voices" are the part of us that is gripped in fear of what change might be like and is scared of the prospect of putting ourselves out there, taking a risk, and trying something new or big.

CHAPTER 8

Prayer I: Praying for Willingness

AT THE END of the previous chapter, we discussed the power and meaningfulness of owning our choice to live spiritually. But, as anyone who has engaged in a process of spiritual development can attest, the initial choice to act, on its own, is not nearly enough to make real progress. The desire and choice to take action is a beginning—but in order to generate the energy and stamina needed to stand up to the challenges that come up, we need to have a level of willingness that permeates our whole self. A superficial impulse to connect to G-d will not be sufficient; we will need a deep wellspring of willingness. Where can we find this? How can we develop it?

One of the most powerful tools for developing willingness is prayer: to turn to our Creator for help in generating a fuller and more sustained willingness to act on our spiritual desires and decisions. At first, this might sound strange. Some of the skeptical thoughts that often come to mind are: "Pray for willingness? What would we pray for? We're either willing or we're not! Even if we were to assume that the power to act is in G-d's hands, the willingness to choose the right thing is surely in ours. Can we really rely upon our Creator to supply the power *and* the willingness to utilize that power? Is that fair? Is it 'permitted'?"

Fortunately, these thoughts are simply incorrect. According to the ancient wisdom of Torah (as well as the contemporary experience of spiritually minded people all over the world), we can and should reach out to G-d for help with willingness. We can ask our Creator, for example: "Master of the world [Father in heaven, higher power of my understanding, etc…], I want to be close to You, but many times I lack the willingness to follow through. Please help me. Grant me sustained willingness to act on my ultimate desire to experience attachment and connection with You."

The ancient wisdom of Torah reveals that the opposing perspective—the one that assumes we cannot ask G-d for assistance with our willingness—actually stems from a dark place of falsehood, a form of egotism. It is an egocentric voice that says, "All the burden rests on you. If you don't have what it takes to sustain willingness or even just open your mouth to pray, the fault lies in you!" If you fall short, it's because you aren't trying hard enough, you're not serious enough, you don't actually care. In reality though, all we are expected to do in life is the best we can for today. The rest—everything else—we leave to G-d. We even rely on our Creator to provide the very willingness required to follow up on our even slight desire to grow.[1]

Why is it OK to ask G-d to grant us unearned willingness? Why would the Creator allow this? Does G-d have to do everything? Don't we have to take some responsibility?

Let's take a look at why we pray through the perspective of the ancient wisdom of the Torah. The very foundation of monotheism is the belief that G-d is perfect and therefore lacks nothing—He has no need for even our genuine prayers. The underlying primary purpose of our prayers is simply the closeness that the request or praise facilitates. Therefore, any lacking in ourselves really represents the opportunity to build further our relationship with G-d. By admitting we need help and then asking for it, we develop connectedness. Prayers are not an act of lethargy—they are acts of humility, honesty, and truth. This wisdom teaches us that our Creator welcomes our prayers for anything, even for willingness and for strength. It reiterates to us that what our Creator wants most for us is connection. If it's what is needed, and we have made our best effort, the

---

[1] "Open up for me an opening like the eye of a needle, and in turn I will enlarge it to be an opening through which wagons can enter" (*Midrash Rabbah*, Song of Songs 5:2).

Creator does not mind driving the bus, being the engine and even the fuel, as long as we make it to the party.

So, we learn that:

- We are enough.
- A willingness to be willing is more than enough to make a beginning.
- The choice itself to grow is valued and embraced, even if it lacks the intensity to carry us through all the way.

We are invited to reach out and connect to our Creator by asking for divine assistance in generating the type of willingness we need to continue on this journey. If we falter in our alacrity and motivation, there is no need for stress; all we need to do is pick up the tool of prayer and ask for renewed spirit, vigor, and motivation to keep going and the strength and feasibility to face blockages—whether emotional or practical—that stand in the way of our progress. We learn that it is not an intensity of willingness that is needed (though we hope for that to develop over time). What we need is a "way of life" that meets the reality on the ground, i.e., an approach or a system that will help us to face the ebb and flow of a spiritual life. Prayer is the key tool that will help us to face our challenges with resilience and to invite our Creator into our process and journey.

STEP 3: WILLINGNESS TO CONNECT— FOSTER WILLINGNESS TO ACT

The question we faced in Step 3 was the degree to which we have an actual willingness to engage a life of conscious contact. In the coming chapters, we will discuss ways of enhancing and further developing our willingness, but we can begin the process of developing willingness even at the point of our choice to continue reading this book.

If we wanted to, we could close this book right now and never give G-d-consciousness significant thought ever again. While developing a conscious relationship with our Creator may very well enhance our spiritual satisfaction and bring great blessing to a person's life, we learned that investing in that is our choice to make. We get to choose if we want it or not. It is critical to enter this process without feelings of coercion by circumstance or guilt. We are not trapped. We have choice, and choosing—even choosing what is best for us—is the great gift our Creator has granted us.

On the other hand, if our response to this question is to keep working at it, stay open-minded to the perspectives and exercises ahead, and have the basic willingness to grow toward conscious contact or even just the willingness to be willing to grow toward conscious contact, we have chosen a life with our Creator. To have success on this journey, we will no doubt need to further develop our actualized willingness. Yet, before we take action, we can start by taking a moment to develop a vibrant willingness and to reflect on the fact of our choice. We can own and acknowledge that we are spiritual people, seeking a spiritual life.

Into Action—Step 3: Willingness to Connect

GETTING RID OF OLD IDEAS AND PRAYING FOR WILLINGNESS

Practice #1: Getting Rid of Old Ideas

This exercise will focus on concretizing our conscious choice to embrace a living relationship with our Creator. We do so by making a verbal statement like:

- "I choose to live consciously connected to my Creator."
- "My Creator, I want to live in conscious connection with You."

To make these statements more real, say them in front of a mirror or to a friend. Sit quietly in meditation and reflect on the choice.

One of the most challenging aspects of the spiritual journey are negative thoughts that come up when we try to move forward. So here, as these thoughts flood in, take note of this resistance. Jot down negative thoughts that come up, such as, "You don't deserve that," "Who says the Creator wants you?" or "But what about that shameful thing you did?" We will call these old ideas—ideas we will have to abandon if we are to experience the success we want.

Take a piece of paper and make a column down the middle. On one side, list the old ideas, taking note that you have the desire and willingness to abandon them. Then, on the other side, write a new idea you would like to develop, one that meets your inner conviction:

- "I don't need to deserve a relationship with my Creator—G-d grants it freely."
- "The Creator is forgiving, patient and tolerant. My Creator embraces me as soon as I return to Him."
- "I am a good person. I have flaws, but I also have many assets and have done many meaningful things. I deserve contact with the Creator."

These are only some examples. We invite you to express new ideas that meet your conviction in writing.

Now, spend a few minutes reflecting on these fresh ideas. Utilizing prayer, ask our Creator to help you embrace these new ideas. Practice mindfulness to head off the old ideas creeping back in. Acknowledge them for what they are. Remind yourself of the new ideas and beliefs you have embraced and which are your truth. Remind yourself that most cynical and pessimistic thoughts come from a low place in your spirit that doesn't represent your full truth.

Verbalize out loud permission to yourself to discard these thoughts in an effort to embrace your actual perspective and attitude. "I am not my thoughts. I sometimes think in a way I don't agree with and I have the right to abandon these thoughts whenever it becomes clear they are not in line with my awareness of truth."

Practice #2: Pray for Willingness

For this exercise, let's give ourselves permission to spend a few days focused exclusively on willingness. Utilizing simple prayer, we can direct our attention toward asking G-d to grant us willingness to move toward and to live in conscious connection. Spend some time reflecting and evaluating whether conscious contact is what you want in your life, and whether you are fully willing to believe it is possible to achieve it. Accept the gift of choosing growth, of deciding firmly that you are going to follow through with your part of applying this approach the best you can, today. Then open yourself to letting our Creator do the rest.

Starting on Day 1, grade your level of willingness from 1–10.

- 1 represents total unwillingness.
- 10 represents total willingness—nothing in the world can stand in your way.

As you move through this practice day by day, check back in and grade your willingness. Don't expect the number to be static or to always move in one direction. It will likely go up and down. The purpose here is to begin to take notice of our level of willingness on any given day and perhaps to begin to detect the subtle shifts inherent in growth. Keep in mind that spiritual development is a process that takes hold over time.

Take three minutes every day during this period to practice meditating on your willingness to connect. Reflect on all the reasons you don't want to. Unearth fears of what a more spiritual life might look like, what outcomes you may not be ready for. Are these fears founded? Are they really true? Ask yourself whether you are willing to be fully willing to grow toward conscious contact. Reflect on the concept that our Creator desires and wills that you beseech Him for assistance in all aspects of this effort. Reflect on the idea that asking for our Creator's help is also a way in which you are living in G-d's will, practicing the faith that G-d will respond to our requests with help and inspiration. Even our requests for willingness to connect are an act on our part to connect. End your period of meditation with prayers of hope and aspiration for the willingness to act on your conviction and to experience the closeness to our Creator that is your destiny.

step four

THERE IS A CREATOR

CHAPTER 9

Keep It Simple: Awareness of a Creator

IN STEPS 1–3, we learned the preparatory stages of spiritual growth. These steps are universal in nature and can be applied to almost any effort to develop and grow:

1. **Be clear about your purpose**: We sought to develop the awareness that we are engaging in a process that is not just a random aspiration—it may be viewed as the fundamental purpose of our spiritual life itself.
2. **Understand the nature of the challenge and develop a hope for achieving our goals**: In this process, this meant developing an awareness that our spiritual aspirations are within our reach, in a real and feasible way.
3. **Develop a strong willingness to act**: This means developing a more established and entrenched desire and willingness to move beyond spiritual fantasy, toward living a truly spiritual life.

Now that we have studied and practiced the tools of primary spiritual purpose, fostering hope, and developing willingness, we are ready to move into the proverbial "meat and potatoes" of this practical action plan.

We will begin this next phase by focusing on firmly establishing in our conscious minds the most simple and fundamental spiritual principle of all: that there is a Creator. In this step, we will focus on building a consistent mindfulness that simply acknowledges that when we speak of developing our relationship with G-d, we mean the Creator of reality. This is not a philosophical exercise. Rather, it is one focused on the development of a clarity and sustained awareness of the convictions and beliefs we already hold.

If you haven't taken time to identify what your current belief is, you can simply ask yourself, "What do I believe?" Often, this seems like a loaded question because maybe we aren't sure, maybe we're wrong, maybe we'll think one thing and then find out later that we don't believe that anymore, and that our previous beliefs were ignorant. Yet, for this exercise, none of that matters. We have engaged a process to begin to develop an experiential relationship with Whatever or Whoever G-d is. In truth, no matter how smart or enlightened we might be, whatever we identify as G-d certainly falls short of the entirety of what the

Creator of all reality is. There is surely more to the Creator than we could ever know. Instead, as we have discussed, we can start from the point we're at right now and use that as the springboard toward spiritual growth. What do I understand G-d/our Creator to be today? It's OK that this understanding will change; in fact, it's more than okay—it's likely inevitable. In this part of the process, we are only looking for a starting point.

To the reader who is unsure of whether there is a G-d, whether they are agnostic or even atheistic, those beliefs are not blocks, either. We—and the whole universe and existence—come from somewhere, and as human beings we get, if we want, to have a relationship with whatever power generated and formed our reality and universe. That is the operation we are discussing here, at least in Step 4: developing an awareness, and thereby a relationship with our Creator, and whether the Creator is called G-d, Hashem, or just Creator, they are at their core one and the same. Here, there is a meeting point between the believer that is sure, the one that is not, and the one who has lost or never had faith. The common point of interest is a move by all toward contact with the Power that created us.

So, where do we begin?

The ancient wisdom of Torah teaches that simple ideas are the ones that our souls most identify with. To better understand this concept, we can reflect on a prayer that Jews say first thing in the morning when they get up. Judaism teaches that the first thing to do in the morning is to thank G-d for blessing us with our souls. According to the Torah outlook, sleep is the time when our deepest essence ascends above the mundane to be recharged and reconnect with its Source. Upon awakening, in the prescribed blessing, we say, "The soul that You granted me is pure." The implication of the wording of the prayer is that our soul, at its core, is pure and simple. Like children, who are simple in the purest fashion, the soul responds to clarity and truth, not complicated intellectualism. Since, in this process of developing G-d-consciousness, we are trying to awaken our soul within, we will focus on speaking its language. The language of simplicity.[1]

For those who grew up in a religious background or have come to a religious conviction along the way, the simple belief in a Creator seems elementary. While our faith may falter, sometimes as a result of negative events in our life, the assertion that we need to reinforce our basic acknowledgment of a Creator will seem far-fetched for many. Even for those of us who are agnostically inclined, there is often at least a basic admission to a belief in some

---

1   *Bilvavi Mishkan Evneh*, part I, p. 39.

kind of creative force in the universe. Those coming from a 12-Step background may feel, "I did this already in Steps 2 and 3 of the 12 Steps when I acknowledged my higher power! I don't need to go back to that again."[2]

---

[2] A note to the reader: We will reiterate that this is not a philosophical book that seeks to prove the existence of G-d or the truth of any particular understanding of G-d. Rather, the goal here, as an expression of our understanding of the book *Bilvavi Mishkan Evneh*, is to present a viable action plan for developing conscious contact and a meaningful relationship with G-d/our Creator, Whoever you understand that to be. The original text of *Bilvavi* spoke to ardently Orthodox Jews with a specific cultural background. Our purpose is to bring those lessons to the wider public because we believe they are broadly applicable to anyone seeking a relationship with G-d/our Creator. We also hope to include some new exercises that will be relevant to the English-speaking audience of spiritual seekers. Nonetheless, we would like to make it clear that it is not our intention at all to prove anything to you, or even to change your mind. Our goal is to present a viable plan that, when put into place, effects real change of consciousness and perspective in a way that enriches one's life with the sense that they have a vibrant relationship with G-d/our Creator, Whoever you understand that to be. In the descriptions above, we spoke of general types of people who are seeking an experiential relationship with the divine. If you are still reading, we assume that includes you—that you want a relationship, or at least want to want one, or are open to wanting one. That is all that is needed to proceed. We hope to provide for you a path that will make it possible to bring that aspiration to fruition in a way that enriches your life and pleases the Creator, Who we believe is waiting for you.

When we think in this way—when our inner voice tells us, "It's silly to spend time on this. I should probably skip forward a little and leave this to the uninitiated"—we are making a grave mistake. We cannot underestimate this juncture of the journey. Success in our mission requires a dynamic awareness of our Creator. We will be working here toward developing a subtle yet electric vibrancy within our consciousness of the most fundamental element of all spiritual growth: awareness of our Creator.

CHAPTER 10

Like You Won the Lottery: "There's Knowing and Then There's KNOWING"

HAVING STATED THAT an electric and vibrant awareness of our Creator is a vital launching point of developing a conscious relationship with G-d, we now need to clarify what that actually means. Aside from throwing ourselves into the depths of philosophical or spiritual works to discover the Creator, what else can we do?

Surprisingly, this kind of deep study is not necessary for our mission at all because, as we already pointed out, complexity and intellectualism will not take us where we want to go.[1] Where, then, do we begin?

---

1 It is important to note that this perspective is not meant to denigrate or devalue the study of spiritual or philosophical texts. The implication here is that the study of such texts enhances our intellectual understanding of our Creator and the universe, but does not replace the necessity for developing experiential comprehensive knowledge by transferring our knowledge, beliefs, and convictions from our

To better understand the process, we must begin by clarifying the objective of this step and what we aim to achieve. While it may be true that we know there is a Creator, what does "know" actually mean? What sort of knowledge about our Creator are we talking about?

Hebrew texts utilize many different terms to describe "knowing" or "knowledge." Each of these terms represents a description of a particular form or origin of knowledge. One Hebrew term that translates as knowledge is *yediah*. This word has two applications or contexts: *yediah sichlit*, meaning purely intellectual knowledge, and *yediah penimit*, meaning internalized knowledge, i.e., experiential or existential awareness.[2] Intellectual knowledge refers to our awareness of a thing in a disconnected way, whereas internal knowledge refers to knowing that thing in an intimate way.

Let's illustrate. Imagine there are two friends, Simon and Levi. One day, Simon and Levi are hanging out and Simon decides to buy a lottery scratch ticket. Incredibly, he wins

---

"minds" to our "hearts." In short, greater intellectual knowledge will enhance the potential of the connection we can experience, but has no bearing on whether real connection is experienced. The knowledge we have right now is sufficient to effect contact; more learning would only enhance that.

2 As defined in *Bilvavi Mishkan Evneh*, part I, p. 43.

twenty million dollars. Simon and Levi each quickly call someone to let them know about this wild turn of events. These people in turn share the good news with others, and before you know it, tens—maybe hundreds—of people all over the world hear about Simon's great fortune.

Now, both Simon and Levi, their family and friends with whom they have shared the news, and everyone that hears about it on social media, all know the same piece of information—that Simon won twenty million dollars. However, you would be remiss to say that they all "know" this information in the same way as Simon. Simon's "knowledge" is much different than Levi's and surely different than that of the many other people who have heard the news. Simon's whole existence is wrapped up in his knowledge. All he can think about is the wonderful things he will do with his wealth. His whole existence has changed.

On the other hand, Levi "knows" Simon won, and he may spend some time thinking about it, but not in the same way as Simon. Even more so, for a further-removed acquaintance, such as a friend of a friend, life will be the same today as it was yesterday, and the same as it will be tomorrow; except that they know of someone who won the lottery.

Simon has a "connected knowledge," while the friend of Levi's friend has a "disconnected knowledge." As we move further away from the source of the information, the knowledge becomes more and more disconnected.

This is precisely what we are looking for here in the fourth step of this process. We are seeking intimate knowledge of the simple idea that there is a Creator. We may "know" that there is a Creator, but do we "know" it like we won twenty million dollars? Again, when we discuss the level of knowledge, we are not talking about a depth of philosophical understanding. We are discussing whether we recognize our Creator on the level that this knowledge is alive within us. Are we aware of it all the time? Does it color how we see everything? This is the type of mindfulness that we will work on—to live simply with our Creator in an experiential way. We want to develop the type of knowledge that is alive—electric. This sort of G-d-consciousness has the power to transform our lives. It allows us to see the world through an entirely new set of lenses. It leads us on a path to a life of conscious contact. Simply stated: **The path to the good life, one lived in conscious awareness of our closeness to our Creator, starts with the comprehensive and intimate awareness that comes along with hitting the jackpot: there is a Creator!**

CHAPTER 11

Tasting G-d

"Taamu u're'u ki tov Hashem—Taste and see that the Lord is good."[1]

IN THE PASSAGE above, the Psalmist, King David, describes encounters with our Creator as tasting and seeing the goodness of G-d. "Tasting" seems like a strange way to describe a spiritual experience. How can we taste our Creator? Even if we were able to experience G-d in a physical way, tasting would hardly be the sense we would use to describe it! Perhaps touch or see or hear, but taste? How would that work?

To begin to understand, let us first retranslate the verse from its original Hebrew into English. Instead of "Taste *and* see," a more precise translation is "Taste *in order* to see the goodness of G-d." In this passage, the Psalmist is teaching us a deep lesson about how to experience our

---

1   Psalms 34:9.

Creator. In order to experience "seeing" G-d, we first need to "taste" G-d.[2]

What, then, is King David referring to when he says to "taste" G-d? If we uncover this secret, it will grant us further clarity on how to incorporate G-d-consciousness into our lives. In truth, "tasting" G-d only seems impossible because our awareness of G-d lies in the intellectual realm. Tasting the divine refers to an experience of our Creator that occurs as one matures their G-d-awareness to a *yediah penimit*, "knowledge of the heart"—a knowledge one feels.

Returning to our analogy of the man who won the lottery, two people can share the same information, but those further removed will have intellectual knowledge, while those who are more personally affected will have more internalized knowledge. The lottery winner himself has the most intense awareness of all. This type of subjective and existential knowledge can be called *yediah sheleimut*, "intimate knowledge."

Knowing our Creator this way is so good, so real, you can "practically taste it." This very modern phrase—"So good I can practically taste it"—captures the essence of what King David meant: an awareness of our Creator that

---

2   *Bilvavi Mishkan Evneh*, part I, p. 48.

is so real, we can almost "see" our Creator's presence in our lives, and we can experience the serene goodness that is G-d-consciousness. This is the sort of awareness we are seeking to develop.

As in the metaphor of the friends and the lottery, intimate knowledge is not generated if the information is limited to the realm of the mind (like the friend of Levi's friend, who "knew" Simon won the lottery). It must also be present in the realm of the heart,[3] the lived and experienced realm (like Simon, who realized his life was forever changed). Without transferring what we know about our Creator in our minds to the realm of our hearts, truly experiential connection cannot be developed. Therefore, we start by developing a simple awareness of our Creator in our intellectual self, and then transfer that awareness to our hearts.

---

3   Knowledge of the heart is a concept that is present in the Five Books of Moses as well as other ancient literature. "Know today and consider in your heart" is a portion of the great soliloquy of Moses before he dies in Deuteronomy 34:5. This is obviously not a reference to the heart as an organ. "Knowing in our hearts" refers to the existential awareness connected to our emotional self and our intuitive sense of things. It is a level of awareness that is more subjective than intellectual awareness. In this way, it can have a greater impact on how we see and experience the world.

In short: **We are seeking to know our Creator in an experiential way.**

As we develop this awareness, we hope to spiritually "taste" G-d in our lives and, as a result, bring to bear this ultimate goodness.[4] This tasting and seeing is essential G-d-consciousness, and it is within our reach. To experience it, we don't need to be great philosophers or even study their works. The secret key to a truly spiritual life is being experientially aware of our Creator, developing a consciousness of G-d that colors our whole perspective, an awareness of our Creator that is personal and real.

Seeing the world through this consciousness will help us foster a life of deep meaning and wholesomeness. "The essence is to know before whom you are striving to grow. At all times and at every moment…the extent to which a person incorporates this awareness into his heart is the extent to which he will experience, on deeper and deeper levels: 'Taste to see the goodness of our Creator.' Experiencing the satisfaction of G-d's presence in this world, now."[5]

---

[4] This correlates with the idea, discussed earlier, that true goodness is the degree to which a thing reveals our Creator's presence in our lives.

[5] This is a direct quote from *Bilvavi Mishkan Evneh*, part I, quoting the great Jewish ethicist and scholar Rav Avraham Yeshaya Karelitz (1878–1953), known as the Chazon Ish.

We are left with a question: What steps must one take to transform intellectual knowledge into experiential/existential awareness? How can we take the awareness of our Creator to the next level, so we can practically taste G-d in our lives and clearly see the goodness?

In the coming chapters we will begin to learn how this can be done simply and systematically. We will include simple and experiential mindfulness exercises to enhance our awareness of the presence of the Creator in our lives.

CHAPTER 12

Transforming Our Hearts

WE NOW NEED to face the most important part of the fourth step in this process: How do we go about "tasting" G-d. How can we transform the simple and basic cognitive awareness we have about our Creator to a level where it can actually be felt?

As we have been demonstrating, this approach is based on a principle of facilitating sustainable spiritual growth. This sort of growth is not achieved as a result of intense efforts that wear us out, leaving us emotionally and spiritually spent. Rather, we achieve sustainable growth through simple actions taken at regular and consistent intervals, with the intention of strengthening and developing our "spiritual selves." Simple messages repeated over and over can have the greatest impact because they speak the language of our souls. When coupled with prayer, they are especially effective at transforming intellectual knowledge to experiential awareness.

There is a famous Jewish tale about Rabbi Akiva of the Talmud. Though he eventually became the greatest

Transforming Our Hearts   101

Jewish scholar and teacher of his time, until forty years of age Akiva was an ignoramus. In fact, Rabbi Akiva later reported that at that point, he absolutely hated scholars and rejected the meaningfulness of a life of study and spiritual pursuits. Akiva was the descendant of converts and was of lower socioeconomic class; as such, he had never had the opportunity to study and resented the intellectual elite. It was his feelings of inferiority and resentment that likely fueled his disdain for the seeming impracticality of a life of service and study.

What changed? How did this ignoramus transform his attitude and go on to dedicate his life to study and the service of his people? How did this angry young man go on to become the greatest Torah teacher of his generation? How did he become the one and only scholar that, as the Talmud states, was able to reach the deepest levels of mystical awareness while keeping his grip on reality?[1]

The midrash describes how one day, Akiva was sitting by a well, and he noticed a hollowed-out stone. He observed that the hole in the stone was created by erosion from small drops of water that were falling onto the rock. Over many years, these small droplets had created a hole. This gave Akiva great inspiration. He realized that his destiny

---

1   Babylonian Talmud, *Chagigah* 14b; Jerusalem Talmud, *Chagigah* 9a.

was not sealed and that no circumstance was fixed, no matter how harsh or unmoving it seemed; even a boulder could be formed and shaped.[2]

Akiva began to look into the deeper meaning of things and went on to become one of the greatest Jewish scholars and leaders in history. What was it specifically that Akiva learned from the rock, and how did this give him the inspiration to radically turn his life around?

To understand, let's analyze the details of the story. Akiva saw the hole in the boulder. What created it? A small drip of water. Each drop of water that fell on the rock was small, weak, and insignificant. Water is one of the softest and most malleable materials in the world, while rock is one of the hardest. What is it that allows the soft and malleable water to erode the hard and fixed rock? Water's strength lies in its consistency. Each drop of water is no different than its predecessor. The first drop exactly resembles the second, and the second resembles the third, and over thousands of years, weak and malleable drops erode hard and powerful rock. Simply put: **It is not the power of the water that shapes the rock but the consistency of the drop.**

---

[2] *Avos D'Rabi Nosson* 6:2.

Let us consider it this way: Even if we took all the water that had dripped over the rock over all those years, and shot it at the rock at one time, it would lack the strength of the consistent small drops to shape the hole in the rock. Propelling this amount of water at the rock with enough force might shatter or crack the rock, but it would never form the exquisite hole created by the slow dripping over time.

This is what inspired Akiva. Perhaps Akiva had regrets over his ignorant life and wanted more meaning, but saw no way out—he did not even know the letters of the *aleph-beis* (Hebrew alphabet). He seemed stuck in his place in society, destined for ignorance. Yet, when he saw the rock, he understood that our hearts, which can feel as hard as rock, can nonetheless change. Akiva thought to himself: *How can I open a heart of stone, that it should be fleshy and alive? Through simple, small drops applied consistently.* The point is simple yet life-changing: **It is not deep thought or intense spiritual experience that will make the real difference.[3] Our effort to take simple, small actions on a regular and consistent basis is what will do the trick.**

---

3   Although for those naturally inclined, these can be a critical element of a vibrant spiritual life.

Through this sort of effort, we can develop our spiritual awareness so that it is alive and vibrant. By simple actions, we can transmit our existing faith from an intellectual knowledge to experiential awareness, and through this we can merit to "taste G-d".

It is important to take a moment to acknowledge one of the most impactful aspects of spiritual development, namely, "sustainable growth." When we use a word like "sustainable," it often conjures up associations of a process that has no failure and no hiccups. When it comes to spiritual development, nothing could be further from the truth. Not only are setbacks an inevitability of spiritual growth, they are also an incalculable gift to the process. We often make the mistake of assuming that a process of positive and uplifting spiritual growth should always feel good and right, and that it should be a consistent upward climb to further perfection. Yet, like many aspects of growth in the universe, spiritual growth looks a lot like an EKG reading, or a chart tracking growth in the stock market: our personal development is full of ups and downs. These ups and downs are not just a reality we must accept. The ancient wisdom of Torah reveals,[4] and contemporary

---

4 Particularly in the writings of Rebbe Nachman of Breslov and the Lubavitcher Rebbe.

experience shows, that the "downs" in the process are not hiccups to be tolerated or survived, but rather, integral parts of the journey. This is true for many reasons, but we will briefly highlight three:

1. Setbacks represent an opportunity to face resistance and challenge and to practice resilience and commitment to the process. This phenomenon actually reinforces growth and also reveals strength that would have otherwise remained dormant. Strength within people is often most acutely expressed when they encounter challenges. Downs therefore represent amazing opportunities to access the spiritual adrenaline that can catapult our growth forward.

2. Downs also provide an amazing opportunity to engage a part of ourselves and a part of our lives that we normally might not associate with spirituality or holiness. We relate spirituality to positive or elevated things. Yet, if all spiritual growth we encountered only felt good, our relationship with G-d and spirituality would be limited. In a human relationship, the most loving and dedicated expression often occurs when things are not going well—when we lean in and stay engaged. Doing so expresses our unconditional commitment to the

bond and connection: "I will love you even when it feels like I don't like you, and that means I love all of you."

3. Turning to those we love for help, nurturing, and affection is a powerfully electric experience. Though we don't wish suffering on ourselves or those we love, when suffering occurs, we are gifted with an incredible opportunity to be vulnerable, to connect, and to feel and give love.

For all these reasons, it is clear that sustainable spiritual growth that includes setbacks and struggles is a wonderful thing. It will entail ups and downs, falling off the beam and getting back on. As Rebbe Nachman of Breslov famously taught: "The whole world [i.e., the entire course of a spiritual process and all of one's life] is a very narrow bridge [i.e., a beam upon which we balance that will include slips and stumbles]; the critical point is never to be afraid [i.e., to trust the process, practice hope and resilience, and get back on when you slip off]."

STEP 4: MEET OUR CREATOR—FACING REALITY

In the fourth step, we looked to begin the process of concretely building conscious contact with G-d. This began with the simplest faith of all: there is a Creator. This was the simple idea that all we see around us stems from one source. As that fact settled in and registered as truth, we could start to see the world through the realization that we are not alone, our lives are not random, and that there is a Creator. There is a beginning that we all share—a source to everything we see.

To foster within ourselves an electric sense of this simple idea, we can begin the practice of simple exercises with consistency. Our strength will not come from the intensity of the spiritual acts but rather from simple, sustained effort that can transform cold intellect into warm and alive experiential and existential awareness. We will no doubt face setbacks and lows along the way. The main thing is to trust the process and stay the course, keeping focused on our mission.

Into Action—Step 4: Meet Our Creator

ACTIVE AWARENESS AND ENGAGING OUR HEARTS

Practice #1: Active Awareness

The objective now is to incorporate a conscious awareness of a creative force in the universe. We will need reminders, so let's set them up throughout the day. Perhaps it's using a reminder feature on your phone or a card in your pocket. Every hour, take one minute to acknowledge verbally, "There is a Creator." Remember not to make it complicated, as that will only get in the way of concrete growth. Close your eyes, take a deep breath, and sit for thirty seconds with the thought that the universe was created by a force. Open your eyes, look around you, and consider the idea that every single detail around you was created by a spiritual force we refer to as G-d.

If we repeat this practice every hour that we are awake, or perhaps just the hours we are active, we will have spent eight to twelve hours in a measure of consciousness of our Creator. Perhaps make the simple commitment to do this practice "no matter what" for a week. Once you have succeeded in doing this for a week, try a month. Those who have been in any sort of recovery or development program know the miraculous effects of doing something consistently for thirty days.[5] So let's give it a try.

---

[5] On a practical level, we must keep in mind the power of an established neural association. The way our brains work is that as we establish good habits of thought and perspective, it becomes easier and easier to maintain the attitudes we want. So whenever we engage an initiative in this area, it is important to remember that there is a beginning, a middle, and an end to the process. To make the process manageable and more pleasant, choose a fixed amount of time and work toward following through for that period. After you are done, evaluate how things are going and choose a follow-up initiative or exercise. Studies imply that about twelve weeks or ninety days is a period that shows real results in establishing a habituated association in our brains. A good suggestion is to break those ninety days into three sections of thirty. While you may not be "perfect" at the initial thirty-day try, you will likely see greater and greater success as you are resilient and stick with the process.

Practice #2: Engaging Our Hearts

Now, to enhance this experience and begin to transfer our awareness from our minds to our hearts, let us add some prayer. This can be done every hour when we pause for reflection—or just a couple of times during the day. Let's consider some examples:

- In the morning, we can practice a simple prayer like this: "Who got me up this morning, and grants me the power to get out of bed? My Creator did. My aspiration today is that I live this day according to G-d's will. Please, G-d, grant me the strength to be a channel of Your light and to keep Your presence in my consciousness all day."
- In the middle of the day, we might pray something like this; "Who created all this stuff around me, the desk in my office (or classroom), the tree that is in front of me? My Creator did. You, G-d, created all of this. Thank You for granting me the gift of life and for Your exquisite creation."

This sort of simple prayer, along with simple reminders and acknowledgments, will help us attain the sustainable spiritual growth and G-d-consciousness that our hearts pine for.

step five

CONNECT WITH CREATEDNESS

CHAPTER 13

A Fully Practical Spirituality

TO RECAP:

- In Step 1, we proposed that *deveikus* (i.e., conscious contact) is in fact the fundamental mission of our lives.
- In Step 2, we then defined *deveikus* as an awareness of the connection with our Creator that inherently exists. By identifying it as something we have that we need to gain awareness of (and not something we need to find or create), we fostered a sense of hope that our spiritual goals are real and within our reach.
- In Step 3, we worked on developing a more vibrant willingness to take action toward achieving a real and sustainable Conscious Connection.
- Finally, in Step 4, we learned about the effort we can make to solidify our basic and simple awareness of our Creator throughout the day. The importance of this step stems from the principle that a simple

awareness of our Creator is the key to opening a spiritual life. We emphasized that the language of our soul is simple and pure, and therefore spiritual development begins with simple and pure ideas.

The next rung in the ladder will involve focusing on the development of our awareness of ourselves as creations. This fifth step in the process seeks to foster a simple and steady mindfulness of our "created-ness"—our place as a valued creation in a created world.

"Really? Do we actually need to spend time working on that? Isn't it pretty obvious to us that we are a creation of something? I didn't create myself!"

There are two ways to respond to this question. The first is related to what we learned in Step 4: Yes, we know we are a creation of something, but do we *know* it? And do we know it *entirely*? Is our awareness like that of the lottery winner or like the distant acquaintance?

The second response is through the ancient wisdom of Torah, which teaches an amazing and novel concept that demonstrates the importance of this aspect of faith. Step 5 is not simply the logical follow-up to Step 4—that once we begin to develop a deep awareness of our Creator, the obvious next step is a developed awareness that we are G-d's creations—rather, this step stands on its own. It is

A Fully Practical Spirituality **115**

an independent and critical step on the journey toward greater spiritual well-being and conscious contact.

To better understand and appreciate this fifth phase of our process, it will be helpful to gain some further clarity on the concept of the inner voice of resistance that we spoke of earlier.

As an illustration of how ego stands in the way of our spiritual development, the ancient wisdom of Torah invites us to reflect on the story of Pharaoh, the Biblical king of Egypt. Maimonides,[1] the famed medieval philosopher and codifier of Jewish Law, calls Pharaoh the "ultimate embodiment of the *yetzer hara*—the inclination to evil.[2] (As we explained earlier, this refers to the part of

---

1   Rabbi Moshe Ben-Maimon (1135–1204), also known as the *Rambam*, was one of the most important Jewish scholars in all of history. As an author, legal scholar, philosopher, medical doctor, and community leader, the impact of *Rambam* to Jewish scholarship, thought, and life, is without equal. *Rambam*'s published works, in their depth and breadth, cover the entirety of Torah law and philosophy. All Jewish scholarship since *Rambam* is compared and contrasted to his thought. The adage that accompanies his fame is, "From Moses to Moses there was no other like Moses," equating his accomplishments and impact to Moses himself.

2   *Rambam* makes this statement in "The Letter of Ethics" to his son, while discussing the ways in which figures from the narratives of the Torah represent archetypal figures representing parts of ourselves. While some have questioned the authenticity of this letter as the

ourselves, as well as the general energy in the world, that is most inclined and attracted to that which creates separation from G-d, i.e., material pleasure, comfort, and sensation for its own sake.) This *yetzer hara* is our ego—the internal voice that tells us we aren't good enough and at the same time that we're too good; that we have no chance of achieving our aspirations, and yet our success is coming to us; that we won't ever be acceptable to G-d, or that G-d simply doesn't care. It is rooted in the part of ourselves that is called "Pharaoh."

In the story of the Exodus, the antagonist, Pharaoh, is a crafty and manipulative king who enslaves the Hebrews. Later on, amazingly, he allows the destruction of his entire country and people when he belligerently resists the command of G-d to "let My people go." In the eyes of the ancient wisdom of Torah, the characters of the Torah narratives are not only historical figures, but also archetypal figures from whom we learn life lessons, and who represent core aspects of our selves. In telling their "stories," the Torah illustrates vital lessons for our lives. As a guide to growth, we are invited to identify the parts of ourselves that these figures represent, with each

---

actual writing of *Rambam*, nearly all major leaders of the schools of Lithuania of the past fifty years consider it authentic.

character representing a potential pitfall to avoid or an ideal to strive for. In this framework, each "villain" of the Torah narrative represents a challenge built into our psyche, while each hero represents qualities to develop and embrace. The message behind the "Inner Pharaoh" is what we are looking for here.

There is a passage in the book of Ezekiel, where the prophet quotes Pharaoh of the Exodus narrative as saying, "I have my river [i.e., the Nile], I made myself [what I am]."[3] Here, the prophet Ezekiel reveals that the great Achilles' heel of Pharaoh (and our Inner Pharaoh) was not heresy, a denial of G-d, but rather an attitude of false self-sufficiency and pride. Pharaoh is king of Egypt, land of the Nile. The Nile afforded ancient Egypt a tremendous advantage over its neighbors. Aside from the ability to transport goods and providing access to fresh water, the Nile represented freedom from the ambiguity of an agricultural system that relied on rain. Having the Nile meant having some measure of control over one's water supply, translating into nearly consistent abundance. In the ancient worldview, a controlled water supply meant there was no need to rely on a deity for basic sustenance. The Nile itself would be your higher power; it didn't

---

3 Ezekiel 29:3.

matter whether the Creator of all the world cared for you or not—His presence was just not necessary in everyday life.

We learn here that the root of our internal resistance to grow is actually the part of us that desperately feels like it needs total self-sufficient independence, without allegiance or loyalty. It does not resist spiritual development because it denies the existence of a Creator, but rather resists growth to avoid our vulnerability as creations. This perspective can be rooted in arrogance and rebelliousness, but it also can be more benign and understandable, as a mechanism of protection from the vulnerability of being reliant on someone or something else, or of being let down. Often, it is both.

Pharaoh, ruler of the land of the Nile, represents the part of us that may accept the idea of a living Creator, but resists accepting the idea that we are creations. This is the source of a disproportionate tendency to fantasize and idolize about being "self-made." This is the illusion: that by ourselves—by our efforts and power alone—we can grow into what we will become, and that we can't rely on any G-d or higher power, or even the support of others. To get "what's coming to us," we will have to take it.

This is the cynical voice of resistance that stands in our way, the real root and source of the internal agnostic that dogs every spiritual step we take. In opposition to humility, gratitude, and acknowledged vulnerability, this inner voice says, "It won't work...you aren't worthy...they're lying...you can't trust the process...you can't really escape the problem..." At the core of our conscious self, we find an ego that is desperate to be self-made. It is an impulse, a denial of our createdness, that subtly strips G-d out of our lives.

Ultimately, this attitude of denial acts as a block to developing a real experience of our Creator. Whether we embrace this attitude from a place of arrogance, aggression, insecurity, or fear, it forces us into a mindset where G-d is only safe, available, and needed in a house of worship or when we are perfect. In that place, spirituality becomes impractical, and our everyday material lives become stripped of G-d's presence.

On the other hand, as we embrace a more holistic view of things, we can begin to welcome our Creator's presence into all aspects of our lives. We know that we are responsible to take action, yet we also need the love and support of a higher power and of others. When we learn to quiet these voices of fear, to reassure our egos that we are in fact *valued* creations and that we are not alone in this world, we are less at odds with everything around us. We begin to see that though we indeed must act in our own interest, "outwit, outsmart, outplay" is not the primary operation of the game of life. The voices of fear and scarcity that scream out for us to prevent every problem that might come up, that see everyone around us as a potential adversary that can ruin our best-laid plans, are quieted. Even though we will surely fall short of perfection, we can rely on our Creator and on others to help us. We can still the thrashing of our ego as it desperately seeks security within itself. We can acknowledge our createdness, that we are part of a greater whole that has a plan and a purpose.

To summarize:

- The ancient wisdom of Torah teaches us that nearly all the struggles we experience in our faith are not actually rooted in a lack of philosophical knowledge or wisdom of G-d, or of how our Creator runs the world.
- Rather, these crises of faith are the outgrowth of a natural resistance to acknowledge the vulnerability of our createdness.
- Our work in the fifth phase of this process is to combat these effects. We aim to focus on creating a strong foundation of faith upon which a life of conscious contact can be built, to invite our Creator's presence into all aspects and facets of our lives, and to create a fully practical spirituality.

CHAPTER 14

Inner Pharaoh—Guerilla Warrior

THE Q&A PRINCIPLE

IN THE PAST chapter, we described the fifth step of this process as the development of an awareness of our createdness, a cognizance of our being creations of a living Creator. We explained that this step is integral to our spiritual growth in order to counteract the impact of an aspect of our basic human nature: our ego or "Inner Pharaoh." In Inner Pharaoh, we identified a part of ourselves that desperately feels the need to deny our createdness as an act of arrogance and/or misplaced self-protection.

What, then, is the work ahead?

- If we believe in the Creator, that G-d created the world and that we didn't just appear on earth spontaneously, what further steps can we take?
- If, as before, the work lies in a simple awareness and not complex philosophy, what else can we do to make strides in this area?

Let's take a look at how the ancient wisdom of Torah teaches us to counteract simple and fundamental blocks in our faithfulness, such as Inner Pharaoh.

To illustrate, let's reflect on one of the most treasured rituals in the Jewish faith, the Passover Seder. The Seder, of course, is the ritual meal on the first night(s) of Passover that includes a recitation of the Exodus narrative. One of the most famous parts of the Seder is the presentation of the Four Questions, "What is different about this night?" and the questions of the Four Sons—the wise son, the wicked son, the simple son, and the son who doesn't know how to ask—which the Torah alludes to in the Exodus narrative.[1] During this juncture of the Seder, the text makes a fascinating statement: "Even if we are all sages…we still must tell over the Exodus narrative in this manner."

Why should a sage who knows the answers still ask the questions and answer them? Isn't this a waste of his time?

From here we derive a dynamic and effective tool that is relevant to this very day. We will call it the Q&A Principle. What is this principle and how does one practice it?

---

1 The wise son, Deuteronomy 6:20–21; the wicked son, Exodus 12:26–27; the simple son, Exodus 13:14; the son who does not know how to ask, Exodus 13:8.

The Haggadah demonstrates that the purpose of asking the obvious questions is to give validation and voice to our inner agnostic, Inner Pharaoh. Then, having heard him out, we give him the simple answers. Just as we give voice to the Four Sons, from wicked to wise, with each receiving a turn to ask their questions, so too, do we allow our own inner voice to ask its questions:

- Why is this night different?
- Is there really meaning to all these rituals?
- Do these rituals have significance to my life?
- Why is life complicated?
- Why do good people suffer?
- What is the purpose of everything?

This concept reveals a remarkable perspective. The cracks in our faith that block our spiritual progress are actually perpetuated by suppressing our inner agnostic voice. When we ignore and suppress Inner Pharaoh, we give his agnosticism power. We enable him to engage in a campaign of spiritual guerrilla warfare unabated.

But, by dragging him out of the subconscious realm and into our conscious mind, these perspectives can be (lovingly) refuted and corrected. When we force him out in the open, the weaknesses of our old ideas are revealed. The power of the question-and-answer type of meditation is similar to that of the inventory process of 12-Step recovery, where there is a focus on writing things down in black and white to flesh them out.[2] Asking what sometimes seems like obvious questions gives validation and light to our old ideas—and repeating to ourselves the simple answers we already know helps demonstrate the folly of these questions. This makes space for us to embrace "new" ideas that are more in line with our convictions and our truths.

In the coming chapters, we will further illustrate how we can utilize this tool to strengthen our spiritual awareness. We can use this tool to begin to repair cracks in our spiritual foundation and foster a spirituality that can withstand the challenges of life with a greater sense of clarity and vibrance.

---

[2] The fourth and tenth steps of the 12 Steps instruct practitioners in developing a habit of intensive and then ongoing written inventory. By putting their feelings and thoughts down on paper, individuals in recovery gain a better understanding of themselves and the circumstances of their lives. This helps to facilitate development in the areas of personal flaws, making amends for past harms, and building a general sense of serenity.

CHAPTER 15

Recognizing Our Createdness— Revealing Inner Abraham

IN THE PAST few chapters, we explained the challenge that Step 5 seeks to address: small cracks in our spiritual foundation. We identified the ultimate source of these cracks as the internal voice called Inner Pharaoh. We demonstrated how our tendency to respond to this agnostic energy through forced suppression is counterproductive. Suppression supplies this part of us with the perfect environment to carry out spiritual guerrilla warfare on our souls, reinforcing old and mistaken negative ideas that erode our spiritual perspective and attitude and ultimately serve as a source for our internal existential conflicts.[1] Because these spiritual challenges are symptoms

---

1 It is important to acknowledge the role that trauma and emotional pain and resentment often play in this aspect of the process. When viewed through an existential and spiritual lens, trauma more than anything else reinforces the old ideas of Inner Pharaoh. "You're not a creation that the Creator cares about," or "There must be no order

of an underlying problem, we must seek to confront the source of the problem rather than just control or remove the symptoms of it. We introduced the Q&A Principle as an antidote specifically for this challenge and generally as a powerful meditative tool to add to our toolbox. The question now is, how can we bring this tool into our lives and into this process?

> to creation or concern for creations—otherwise why would pain like this exist?" These and many other such feelings and conclusions are the natural result of encountering pain and unfairness. Processing and healing emotional pain are often critical prerequisites to making substantial progress in quieting the voice of Inner Pharaoh. Development of faith can be useful in this process, but more often than not, the guidance and support of a trained mental health professional is critical to any viable success at healing the pain of traumas, particularly those that occurred in childhood. It is also important to point out that the existential aspects of the effects of trauma may also often be ignored or overlooked. Comprehensive treatment of trauma most often includes addressing its effects in a comprehensive and holistic manner that addresses all aspects, including the existential and spiritual. We encourage the reader to seek out experienced and/or qualified persons to process thoughts and feelings related to trauma. Working on spirituality often highlights this sort of emotional baggage. The identification of post-traumatic stress reactions or other impacts of trauma is a meaningful opportunity to identify and ultimately flesh out these painful aspects of our lives. Again, this is best and most safely accomplished with someone trained, experienced, and qualified in the intervention and treatment of trauma.

The power of this technique is that by asking simple questions and giving answers, we access another part of ourselves that is illustrated in the characters of the Torah, which we can refer to as "Inner Abraham." Abraham was raised in the house of idolaters. His community had forgotten the Creator and preached a spirituality rooted in the worship of false idols. Young Abraham rejected this worship. In his quest for truth, he searched out nature and the world around him and eventually recognized a singular Creator and divine power.

Following in Abraham's footsteps, by revealing the Inner Abraham within our souls, we will begin seeking the Creator through observing creation around us. Inner Abraham is the antidote to Inner Pharaoh. Even though our experience of life might be very different from historical Abraham, the concept of approaching nature to see the Creator puts us in touch with our Inner Abraham. Inner Abraham represents the simplest and purest parts of our souls. By giving life to this part, we fill the cracks in the foundation of our faith.

STEP 5: CONNECT WITH CREATEDNESS—ACCEPTING OUR VULNERABILITY

In Step 5, we moved away from Who G-d is and toward our awareness of who we are and what the world around us represents. We learned that drawing focus to our createdness and the inherent vulnerability that comes along with that triggers an inner reaction—we resist admitting we don't have control and having to acknowledge what we have could be taken away at any time. We defined this reaction, and the part of ourselves that causes it, as Inner Pharaoh, and saw how it acts as an emotional block between us and our Creator. We learned that we need to activate Inner Abraham to break free of this challenge and accept our Creator into our lives. In short: **Inner Abraham is the antidote to Inner Pharaoh.**

Inner Pharaoh is the voice that resists the vulnerability of an acknowledged createdness, and Inner Abraham is the pure and curious aspect of our soul. We learned that by giving life to this part, by looking for our Creator in the creation around us, we can quiet the voice of Inner Pharaoh and open the door to conscious connection.

Proceeding in this effort will entail a three-part campaign of beginning to remove the natural denial of our createdness:

1. **The createdness of everything around us**: an awareness that all we see around us is a creation of our Creator.
2. **Our personal createdness**: an awareness that we are creations of the Creator.
3. **Createdness of "now"**: an awareness that everything that unfolds around us is a creation.

Having made progress, we will be more prepared to embrace a life perspective that sees everything around us as a constant manifestation and unfolding of creation itself. We will begin to view all that occurs around us as the continued outflow of creation and of its Creator.

Into Action—Step 5: Connect with Createdness

THE Q&A PRINCIPLE AND IN THE NOW
Practice #1: The Q&A Principle

The tool of Q&A is essentially a meditative practice, but it is slightly different than other practices we have discussed, and in some ways an easier form of meditation and reflection for those new to this sort of discipline. As we will see, this meditation/reflection includes a verbal exercise, which may at first feel strange. Let's be brave and try something new, or perhaps, as we see from the Passover Seder Haggadah, something ancient.

The first part will be a reflection of an awareness of **the createdness of everything around us**. This includes being mindful that everything around us is a creation of our Creator. To begin, we simply reflect on anything we see around us and ask ourselves:

- "Where did these things come from?"
- "Where did those trees come from?"
- "Where did those rocks come from?"
- "Where did the moon come from?"
- "Do things create themselves?"

The answer we would give for all of these questions is that obviously none of these things could have created themselves; all were created by something, i.e., a Creator of some kind.

In this exercise, we are inviting ourselves to see the presence of our Creator all around us.

Interestingly, these specific reflections don't necessarily have to relate to the nature of our *interaction* with our Creator, as might be the case when coming from a religious perspective. In this first reflection, we are merely bringing to mind the reality of the createdness of all things around us, as opposed to the active involvement of the Creator in our present reality. This is not said as validation or denial of our Creator's omnipresence. It is affirmation that in attempting to quiet the voice of our ego, we can recognize that no matter what our conception of our Creator is, we are all, plain and simple, emanations of that Creator. We then become more humble and develop a greater sense of unity with that which is around us.

The next phase in this process is an awareness of **personal createdness**. For this, we employ the same meditative practice and reflections as before, but apply them to ourselves:

- Starting with our bodies, we say, for example, "Who made this arm? Did it develop on its own?

No, the Creator designed it and created a mechanism for its formation."
- "Who created the fact that I prefer vanilla over chocolate ice cream? It was our Creator who willed it to be just that way."
- "Who created my natural disposition for writing, my instinct to lean in when things get most panicked, or to project fears when things seem to be fine for now? Did that all develop out of random chance? No, it was planted and planned that way by our Creator."

In this way we reflect how each part of us, physically and spiritually, is a product and creation of our Creator. By doing this, we seek to establish in our hearts, in a simple and experiential way, that we are creations and quiet our ego's fearful voice of resistance.

The last phase of this effort is the **createdness of *now***, an awareness that everything that is unfolding around us is an emanation of our Creator.[2] Questions and answers at this phase might look like this: "Who organized life so that I am living this moment at this juncture of history?

---

[2] In contrast to our comment earlier, this specific reflection is clearly more closely aligned with the theological perspective of the omnipresence of an active and living Creator/G-d/Higher Power.

Taking into account all the moments that have occurred throughout all of human history and world history and time itself, this moment—where I am in reflection and awareness of reality—who chose it? It was my Creator. G-d, You planned this moment for me, for us to experience together." This form of reflection and prayer really takes concepts like "living in the now" to a new level. It invites the Creator into our minds, hearts, and conscious experience in a vibrant and electric way.

These three forms of meditation can be practiced, one at time, over a period of time.

For a weekly plan:

- Week 1: Spend a few moments each day developing awareness of the creation around you.
- Week 2: Spend a few moments each day developing awareness of your personal createdness.
- Week 3: Spend a few moments each day developing awareness on living with G-d in the now.

Alternatively, you can do all three practices within one week:

- Days 1–2: Spend a few moments developing awareness of the creation around you.
- Days 3–4: Spend a few moments developing awareness of your personal createdness.

- Days 5–6: Spend a few moments developing awareness of living with G-d in the now.
- Day 7: Practice reflecting upon all three.

If daily meditation doesn't work for you, weekends may be a time when you are more relaxed and have more time to focus on these practices. Try reflecting on each of these three areas in depth for a few weekends in succession.

Finally, you can choose three different times over a single weekend to work on each meditation.

The main objective is to develop the meditative practice that works for you and honors your commitment and right to a vibrant and meaningful relationship with our Creator.

Practice #2: In the Now

We have been talking a lot about developing a simple practice of meditation in our day. The types of meditation we have discussed are essentially composed of the combined practice of consistent awareness exercises along with the practice of deep reflection. Throughout this process, we have alluded to these two types of exercises:

- **Consistent awareness** entails focusing on developing a simple and regular awareness of the particular area or phase we are working on.
- We complement this awareness through **deep reflection**—setting aside time in the day or week to reflect on this area, phase, or concept in more depth.

Before we move on, it will be useful to review and to spell out this process in greater detail.

With consistent awareness exercises, we train ourselves to regularly think about spiritual matters in a simple and down-to-earth manner. As we practice this, a spiritual perspective will become more like second nature. Incorporating whatever new perspective or attitude we are developing into our consciousness does not require interrupting our day. Rather, we can set up simple reminders that relate to what we are working on at any given time, which will allow us to draw our perspective back to our spiritual beliefs when we find ourselves going off-course. This practice does require some fortitude, but just enough to take a few deep breaths at different points in the day for making some time for these acknowledgments. We give ourselves the opportunity to put other pressing matters aside for just a few moments in order to welcome in a spiritual perspective.

The next aspect is deep reflection, and this requires more than just setting aside a moment to refocus. At first, it might entail two to five minutes, but as you develop your abilities, you may spend twenty minutes or more to reflect deeply on the spiritual concepts you are working on. The difference here is more depth but less frequency. This could involve daily practice for some and just once a week for others. No matter how we proceed, it is critical that we grant ourselves the gift of time to focus on the things that are important to us. This process will at first be uncomfortable, perhaps foreign, but eventually we will find it to be the most relaxing and rewarding time of our day (or week!)—a time that truly reflects self-investment and care.

Therefore, we will continue the work of Step 5 by utilizing the practice of conscious reminders and intensive reflection. We can start by plugging in to the three areas of awareness we worked on with the Q&A Principle.

First, let us focus on developing an awareness of the createdness of everything around us. As part of our consistent awareness practice, we can work on developing a discipline of drawing our attention to this area and concept in the kind of hourly intervals we practiced in the earlier Steps. This means taking a moment each hour to look at everything around us and ask ourselves, "Who created this?" Then, we can give the obvious answer, "The Creator did." It's as simple as that. After this develops into second nature (meaning, we begin to notice ourselves naturally thinking this way[3]), we can move on to developing

---

3   Note: Our ability to generate this sort of shift in our perspective is not some deep, mystical, otherworldly sort of thing. The ability for us to consistently look around and have cognizance of the createdness of everything around us, with just subtle and minimal reminders, is simple neuroscience. With practice, we can develop neural pathways that direct our brains to naturally and pleasantly have simple types of mindful awareness of spiritual ideas. These don't require thinking power or focus. Rather, we can train our minds to look through a new lens; it's just the mechanics of how our brains work. This won't work as easily or at all with complex and multilayered ideas—but with simple ones (as with any muscle memory development), it's just a matter of repetition, practice, and time. It's also important to remind ourselves that we aren't attempting to be spiritual gurus or have superpowered vision of spirituality. It's just a matter of developing a simple and sustainable cognizance of our spiritual beliefs.

a greater awareness of our personal createdness, and then the createdness of the current moment.

Next, we will continue with a deep reflection practice. We can set aside time—whether five minutes, half-hour or whatever works for us—daily or weekly, to sit down quietly, without distractions, and think deeply about the createdness of everything around us. After a few sessions of deep reflection in this area, we will follow the same steps, focusing on our personal createdness, and then the createdness of the moment we are in.

As a practical suggestion for setting aside this time, choose a time when other things won't get in the way. Giving priority to deep reflection often entails picking out a time when there is quiet in your life. This entire practice is a spiritual one, rooted in G-d's will for you, so consider carving out a time that you are already dedicating to spiritual disciplines. If you are a religious person, for example, take the first five minutes of the time you use for religious prayers to sit quietly and reflect on your beliefs and convictions. If you are in a recovery program, why not spend five minutes at the beginning or end of a recovery meeting sitting quietly by yourself and reflecting on your spiritual work.

As this work continues, we become more and more prepared for the sixth step in our process: awareness of the divine hand in every aspect of our lives. We will work on developing a practical and down-to-earth cognizance of our Creator's omnipresence in our lives in a vibrant and real way.

step six

G-D IS IN CHARGE

CHAPTER 16

How "In Charge" Is G-d?

WE STARTED THIS process by clarifying the mission ahead and solidifying our acceptance and willingness for conscious contact with our Creator. Then, we were reintroduced to "G-d," so to speak, as Creator of our reality, and then to ourselves, and everything around us, as creations.

The next phase will reflect on the extent of our involvement with G-d, what our relationship might look like in real time, today. Creation was then—what about now? What can the extent of our relationship to Him possibly be?[1]

---

[1] All of the ideas we will discuss in this step are based on a number of fundamental premises: (1) Our Creator, the source of all that occurs, remains present; (2) our Creator *wants* what's best for us; and (3) our Creator *knows* what's best for us, even though the plan is sometimes mysterious or outside our comprehension. Because this is not a philosophical book, we will not discuss sources or proofs for these ideas at all. Basic spiritual philosophy (including those rooted in religion and those not) hold these to be true in some form or another. Though different philosophies take varying approaches to understanding these premises, all these spiritual disciplines, which have the goal of

The spiritual lens of conscious contact that we have been working to develop enables us to experience every detail of our lives as under the constant and present influence of our Creator. This process of spiritual growth will encourage us to develop a clear mindfulness and experiential awareness of this idea. The work of the sixth step will be to revitalize our awareness of our Creator's omnipresence in our lives.

HOW SERIOUS IS IT?

Recognition of the influence of a higher and conscious force directing our lives can be separated into two categories:

---

an intimate relationship with our Creator, share these fundamental ideas. Therefore, moving forward we will speak from this premise and invite the reader to explore further according to their conscience and in sources they are comfortable with.

Even so, if the idea of a present and loving higher power is not within your conviction, you may encounter challenges with this step. We therefore invite you to either absorb the concepts ahead that fit your conviction—i.e., take what you like and leave the rest—or turn back and focus on the previous steps, which do not require the perspective of a present and actively involved G-d in your life. We mean this in the most accepting and nonjudgmental way possible, while at the same time maintaining confidence and belief, without apology, in a caring, present, and engaged Creator.

1. **Significant**: who and when we might marry, where we might live, how we will make a living, how we will face an overwhelming challenge, etc.
2. **Seemingly inconsequential**: These are often the aspects of life that are constant and regular, and it is easy to forget that they are being directed by a higher and conscious force.

When developing spiritual awareness, it is easier and more natural to recognize our Creator's influence in the more significant aspects of life. It is often easier, for example, to seek divine assistance when we are engaged in significant things or problems, such as seeking a mate, a job, or the right house. When we encounter areas outside our immediate "control" or influence, when we are more obviously vulnerable, seeing the presence of a higher force, or hoping for one, seems like our only choice. In such situations, we are naturally more open-minded about using our free will to connect with our Creator, and our usual resistance is reduced.

But in times when things are going right and as expected, it is much easier to forget about the directive force that is accompanying us on our journey. When things go smoothly and we show up on time, or things work out pretty much the way we had planned or hoped, it is easier to feel like we are in control or at least know what to expect from the system.

Simply put, in life, we are more often faced with things that make it easier to forget G-d than those that remind us of G-d's presence. So, as we seek to develop an awareness of our Creator in real time, the "regular" areas—the stuff that "encourages" us to forget G-d's presence—become vitally important. These, for the most part, represent the normal comings and goings of our lives and are what we deal with most often.

In order to begin to live with our Creator in a vibrant and present way, we will strive to see and acknowledge our Creator in *every* area and decision of our lives, especially the ones that subtly make it seem like our Creator is just not around or needed. This will be the focus of the next leg of our journey.

CHAPTER 17

Transforming Our Hearts: Spiritual Speech

IN SEEKING CONSCIOUS connection with our Creator, we are looking for a sense of vibrant awareness of our Creator. To develop this awareness, we have some work to do. An intellectual acknowledgment of G-d's presence as the operator of all existence will simply not be enough to accomplish the task. We will need to go deeper.

To gain substantive mindfulness of the omnipresence of our Creator, we will begin by trying to reduce any additional ego-driven resistance. The ancient wisdom of Torah teaches that the term "foreskin of the heart" (Deuteronomy 10:16) refers to a blockage that prevents what we know from penetrating our hearts to create existential change. To effectively evolve and grow, we must remove these blockages. This as yet undefined blockage is often driven by a different aspect of the ego we described earlier. Earlier, we described the aspect of our ego that resists acknowledgment of our createdness and fears admitting where we come from and that we are creations of a Creator. At this juncture of our spiritual work, we will attempt to reduce a similar but more advanced aspect of the same impulse: an obsession with seeing ourselves as in charge, as the Boss of our lives. This impulse resists admitting that our Creator is present and engaged in our lives, not only because admitting we are creations means we are subject to G-d's power, but that our Creator's influence and awareness of His will becomes a present and viable consideration.

There are two phases to reducing and combating this impulse and developing mindfulness of the omnipresence of our Creator:

1. The first involves the type of meditative and mindfulness exercises we have been discussing throughout. Here, in the sixth step, to grow efficiently, we can set aside times throughout the day to think simply about this particular area, perhaps by setting ourselves reminders every hour or so. We could couple this with practice of deep reflection at less regular intervals. These types of exercises will be most helpful in developing further awareness of the omnipresence of our Creator.
2. The second useful tool will be to begin utilizing the power of speech to effect growth from within.

The ancient wisdom of Torah reveals that the spoken word, harnessed as a spiritual tool, has a deep and powerful ability to penetrate the innermost areas of our hearts. As part of this process, we will also begin to speak to G-d, not only in the third person as an impersonal prayer, but rather to begin to relate to our Creator in a very intimate and personalized way. By opening this new pathway, we will have a powerful tool that can help combat the forces of resistance that dog our progress.

So, what is *spiritual speech*, and how does one develop it?

By spiritual speech, we specifically mean the use of speech as an intermediary between the mind and the heart. This concept is introduced in Psalms 116:10, when King David states: "I believe, because I speak."

The practice of spiritual speech is to regulate ourselves to speak out words of faith on a regular basis. This has two applications. The first involves speaking in a manner that expresses and promotes our faith and spiritual awareness. Throughout our day, we can incorporate and practice words of faith. Even if these ideas are not fully entrenched in our consciousness, we can still practice speaking in a manner that reflects what our core faith or conviction is, or even just to affirm what we aspire our faith to be. By doing this, these "truths" become rooted deeper and deeper into our consciousness. This can be as simple as repeating the terms "Thank G-d" or "G-d willing," or any similar type of speech. By doing this purposefully, we affirm our convictions and faith, and affirm our belief in our own growth in the process of developing vibrant conscious contact.

Still, just saying "Thank G-d" or "G-d willing," etc., can be superficial. The second application elaborates further on what a more meaningful, deep, spiritual, and faithful manifestation of speech might look like. It would entail making the effort to actively speak words of faith as a form of mantra. We could take the concepts we have reflected upon and speak them out in a clear and simple manner, while going about the practical aspects of our lives. This can also involve talking to—and not just about—our Creator.

To further elaborate, communication in general, with anyone, has two distinct levels. One level is a more passive or closed type, while the other is open, intimate, and straightforward. This same frame holds true in our dialogue with G-d:

- When we talk to G-d in a closed manner, we might speak in the third person. For example, we might say, "G-d designated that I have this relationship with this person or that this be my home."

- When communicating in an open manner, we speak to G-d in the first person, as if our Creator is right there with us. For example, "You designated that this relationship be in my life, that this house should be my home."

When practicing spiritual speech, the optimum is open and direct dialogue. The relationship we desire to build with our Creator is one that is open and in the first person, and our dialogue with Him should therefore reflect that ideal. In order to accomplish this, we will have to get used to communicating openly and in a friendly manner. This practice may initially be uncomfortable, and if third-person dialogue is easier, perhaps start there. But eventually, the goal is to have a relationship with our Creator that is intimate and personal.

In this chapter, we have begun to introduce the spiritual tool of speech. In the coming chapters, we will highlight more of the practical applications of this tool in our lives. Through continued practice, we will begin to sense the kind of pivotal role that speech can play in our spiritual development. Our species is distinguished from others by our ability to speak. Our power of speech is a vital medium for communication and connection, both with other people and with our Creator. Speech can act as a medium to develop our hearts and our spiritual consciousness. But, before we move on to fully explore spiritual speech and its applications, we will first take what may seem a slight detour to reflect on the role of anger and resentment in holding us back from vibrant awareness of G-d's role in our lives. As we will discover, the awareness we will gain from discussing these topics will ultimately help us to incorporate a present Conscious Connection into our lives.

CHAPTER 18

Anger, Frustration, and Resentment

THERE IS A common saying in 12-Step recovery circles: **Expectation is the mother of all resentments.** Furthermore, resentments are identified in those programs as the most dangerous to our emotional balance and spiritual serenity. The ancient wisdom of Torah teaches that when we break down anger and resentment to its bare bones, we find a lack of acceptance and faith.[1]

---

1   It is important to state clearly that discussing the role of *emunah* (faith) in relation to our feelings about past hurts is not meant to diminish the impact or seriousness of resentful feelings related to traumatic events, especially those from childhood. Often, these connected-but-separate aspects of a singular challenge are conflated. When the focus on faith and spirituality is emphasized while feelings and emotional needs are ignored, this acts to invalidate the pain of those who have encountered major and complex life traumas. As if more faith *should* solve what is a serious facet of emotional pathology. Though an aspect of resentments related to major and complex trauma relates to faith and spirituality, much of it does not. The discussion in these chapters does not include, nor does it replace, the need for processing trauma with

To better understand the impact and role of anger and frustration in the process of spiritual development, let's simply ask: Why do people get frustrated and/or angry? The triggers of frustration can be broken down into two primary sources:

1. **Unfulfilled will**: Our will or expectation is that such-and-such *should* happen or that so-and-so *should* behave in a certain way. When that sequence doesn't play out, we become frustrated. That frustration can be expressed emotionally as anger, and/or held on to as resentment.
2. **Honor or ego**: When we believe that a certain type or level of honor is owed to us, and it is not, we get frustrated, become angry, and ultimately resentful.

Let's further break down these categories to help illuminate our point. Within each of these categories of anger are two types of triggers. The first type of trigger is when something occurs, not as the result of actions taken

---

the help a trained professional. With that said, processing traumas in a therapeutic environment does not replace the necessity to process the impact of that trauma on one's spirituality and faith. When people engage both spiritual and clinical channels in their process of healing, the results are electric and powerful, and should be valued, respected and cherished by all.

by a particular person, but rather as part of the natural order of things. The second is when a specific person, or group of people, intentionally and purposely impacts our desired outcome.

The primary difference between these two triggers is that in the latter type, when our frustration is caused by a person or persons, our anger can be directed at whomever seems responsible. In the first type, however, there is no destination for our feelings. This can make things complicated.

Let's illustrate: a person on his way to work gets a flat tire and becomes frustrated, so he angrily bangs the steering wheel and curses his circumstances. If we were to ask him at that moment, "Who are you upset at? The tire? The steering wheel? The dashboard?" he would surely laugh at himself and admit, "No, I'm not angry at the car. I'm just frustrated at the situation."

The truth is, though, that his feelings of frustration and the accompanying anger have no appropriate destination. He is left with nothing but the feelings of frustration at his "situation," which really means at nothing. For the purpose of our discussion, let's call this trigger *undirected anger/frustration*. We will call the other type *directed anger/frustration*.

When reflecting on these from a spiritual and faithful perspective of an ever-present Creator, both types of triggers have one ultimate cause, and therefore one destination for expression: G-d. If we think about it, who is ultimately responsible for the events that occur in our lives? If we believe that "everything happens in G-d's world for a reason," whether it came about through the free-willed choice of another person or not, our Creator co-signed that this could happen to us. Therefore, when we get frustrated and become angry, on the deepest (and most subtle) level, we are also angry at our Creator. Obviously, it is not our goal, nor is it conducive to a spiritual life, to walk around angry at and resentful of G-d! But if we want to improve and enhance our relationship with our Creator, it is essential for us to be honest with ourselves about our feelings. If we don't internalize this basic fact, we might spend our lives misdirecting our anger and resentment, never truly letting them go. If we don't face this "fact" of the faithful perspective—that our Creator is just as responsible for the things we don't like as for the things we love—and develop the skills to process our disappointments, we won't ever be able to incorporate an actual awareness of G-d's omnipresence into our lives. We will always be subtly dogged by the dark or painful aspects of our lives, which reinforce the feeling that our Creator isn't really fully there.

Anger, Frustration, and Resentment **157**

Therefore, before we move on, we will spend some time processing these different forms of frustration and our sometimes angry and resentful reactions. In the end, we will discover that these most challenging disappointments are actually a treasure trove of opportunity to further develop our relationship with G-d and acknowledge our Creator's active role in our lives.

CHAPTER 19

G-d's Way or My Way: Inner Bilaam

IN THE PAST chapter we broke down our reactions to frustration into two categories: undirected anger/frustration and directed anger/frustration. We explored the precipitators of frustration:

- When a circumstance plays out that is contrary to how we feel it should be
- When the expected level or type of respect that we feel is owed to us is not shown

Let's explore how a more developed life of faith could serve as an antidote to both of these challenges. We will begin with undirected anger, and discuss directed anger in the coming chapter.

Previously, we used the metaphor of a person driving a car who gets a flat tire and becomes angry. When asked about where his anger is truly directed, we saw he was likely to answer that his true anger was at the situation, not at the car or its components. This is a classic example of undirected anger. We often make efforts to do the "right" thing, and along comes some happenstance that impedes our progress. This can be incredibly frustrating, sometimes enraging. This sort of challenge is actually described in the Torah in the narrative of Bilaam, the evil prophet who sought to curse the Israelites.[1] In the story, Bilaam's famous talking donkey won't stop veering off the road and Bilaam simply loses it. Let's look at the story and see what we can learn about the use of faith in navigating the impulse toward undirected anger.

As we discussed earlier, in the eyes of the ancient wisdom of Torah, the Torah narratives are not only historical events, but rather precious life lessons. The villains and heroes of the Torah represent parts of ourselves that we must correct or foster in the journey toward spiritual fulfillment. In this chapter, we will turn to the villain Bilaam within us.

Bilaam was a prophet of similar stature to Moses. Jewish tradition describes his involvement in the wars between the tribes of Moav and Midian. As the Israelites approach the Holy Land after their forty-year journey in the desert, these two enemies join forces to prevent the Israelites from reaching their destination. The Midianites approach

---

1   Numbers 22:2–24:25.

their prophet Bilaam to curse the Israelites so that they can successfully wage war with Israel. They promise riches and glory to Bilaam if he is triumphant. The only problem for Bilaam is that G-d does not allow him to curse the Israelites. Eventually, after multiple requests by Bilaam to join them, G-d acquiesces to his request but warns him to only say what he is instructed to. Bilaam sets out on his favorite donkey for the journey, and the narrative informs us that his inner intention was a hope to sway G-d to his own prerogative and agenda: to curse the Israelites.

Unfortunately for Bilaam, his donkey does not cooperate. As they ride along, Bilaam's donkey veers off the path, and as many times as Bilaam tries to redirect his normally trusty steed back onto the road, it continues to veer off. Eventually, at a narrow pass, the donkey presses hard into a retaining wall, pinning Bilaam's leg against the rock. The next time the donkey veers from the path, Bilaam becomes enraged and begins to mercilessly beat the donkey, who then miraculously talks, complaining to her master that she is always trustworthy and faithful. "Why would you beat me, master?" Bilaam is shaken by the miracle and suddenly becomes aware that an angel of G-d was actually standing in the road wielding a sword and had been there the whole time. The angel was spooking the donkey all along, and that's what had caused the erratic behavior. His

G-d's Way or My Way: Inner Bilaam 161

donkey was, in fact, protecting him from the angel, who was sent by G-d to remind Bilaam to remain aligned with G-d's will and not try and manipulatively exert his own.

It is clear from the story that the donkey itself was not choosing to impede Bilaam's path; rather, the actions of the donkey were the outgrowth of G-d's engagement with Bilaam. As we mentioned, Bilaam became enraged and beat his donkey. In the modern allegory, he slammed the steering wheel. He only stopped his raging when the donkey spoke, and this shook him to a new perspective, making him aware of the divine nature of the detours.

Let us take a closer look at this story and see how it contains exactly the lesson we are looking for. Bilaam, himself an enlightened prophet who spoke directly with G-d, became entangled in an underhanded plot to destroy the Israelites. To accomplish his dastardly plan of bringing about the defeat of the Israelites, he sought to curse them. Yet, Bilaam understood that he could not accomplish anything without G-d's permission. When reviewing the story, it becomes clear that there came a point when Bilaam's greed and desire for honor and glory colored his view of reality. His perspective shifted away from staying within the lines of G-d's will to a fixation on the fulfillment of his own agenda. Bilaam, in his state of willfulness, sees the donkey's disobedience as a personal affront to his honor and as a roadblock to the fulfillment of his desire. When the donkey veers off the road, and in the ensuing struggle crushes Bilaam's leg, Bilaam is enraged and eventually begins to beat her. The truth is, even when the donkey first speaks to him, Bilaam is so wrapped up in his own willfulness, he begins to argue with the animal. It is only when his eyes are "opened" to the reality of the sword-wielding angel that he is shocked back into a mindfulness of G-d and truth-centered attitude.

What was it that triggered Bilaam's episode of misdirected rage? He didn't see the angel. Had Bilaam seen the angel all along, he would have understood his donkey's misbehavior and would never have become upset. In other words, had Bilaam been attuned to the spiritual reality, he might have recognized that G-d was indeed trying to save him from making a terrible mistake.

We might ask, however: "If G-d 'closed' his eyes to seeing the angel, Bilaam couldn't actually control what he saw. So what could he have done to prevent it?"

The analogy here invites us to look deeper into our underlying motives, which block us off from truth. The problem wasn't that Bilaam didn't see the angel. Not seeing the angel was merely the outcome of his bad choice. The problem was how Bilaam began his trip in the first place. Bilaam was wrapped up in his own plans and designs. If Bilaam had maintained a humbled intention and perspective going in, he never would have been closed to the reality of the angel at all. A proper attitude of faith could have saved him from the whole negative experience.

The analogy here is to our own lives, to notice how often we are closed off from seeing the truth because we are too wrapped up in what we decide the outcome should look like. The angel in the metaphor is not referring to some kind of mystical force; it's referring to the mainstay of a faith-oriented perspective. Faith allows us to surrender the outcome and focus on right action and effort. When we are free of preconceived expectations of what the outcome of life is supposed to be, what should happen, and what we deserve, there isn't room for rageful reactions to our frustrations.

When we say faith is an antidote to resentment, we are not referring to the use of faith as a tool to suppress unwanted and non-sensible anger, for example, by saying to ourselves, "I would be angry, *but* I believe G-d is in charge so I'll just tell myself to stop feeling that way." Anger suppression, as a rule, only causes further anger and resentment or sends the anger into the unconscious where it can do significant damage to our contentment, well-being, and relationships. Rather, by developing a vibrant mindfulness of faith, our anger and resentment naturally weaken, and are often headed off before taking hold at all. If we practice and improve this kind of conscious relationship with G-d, it becomes harder for resentment to take a foothold. When it does occur, it can be much more easily expelled.

Briefly speaking, the most effective approach for addressing frustration, anger, and resentment that we experience is to first reduce reactionary emotions and behaviors. The goal is to disengage from a negative loop or pattern that occurs when we feed into feelings of self-righteousness and indignation. We need to take steps to process our feelings about what occurred, the impact and outcome the situation had on our lives, what our part was, and how we were affected and harmed.

The approach then, is to take steps that allow for healing. Healing is accomplished through talking out the anger and developing a practice of forgiveness and acceptance. Sometimes, healing occurs naturally over time. However, often—especially when it comes to intensive trauma, such as childhood traumas—this sort of healing requires specialty treatment.[2]

---

[2] Much has been written about this topic and is readily available for those who are interested.

Returning to our original example: If we consistently spend even a few moments doing some quick G-d-consciousness exercises before getting in the car and heading out to work and incorporate regular practice of deep reflection and faith-oriented speech meditation into our schedules, then when the tire blows, our natural response may no longer be overt anger, but acceptance. If our mindset is consistently oriented toward being a channel of our Creator's will, it won't matter as much if unforeseen delays prevent us from making it to our appointment on time. If we have done our part to leave on time, taking note of the regular traffic patterns, we don't need to stress. We can calmly state: "If G-d wants me here at this moment in this circumstance, that's just fine with me." Our focus can be more easily directed toward usefulness to our Creator and others, in a manner that is practical, not just theoretical. In this example, being late and stuck might mean we have time to reach out and call someone to see how they are doing, or it might give us the opportunity to develop empathy and compassion for those who have affected us with their lateness.

For this reason, the extent to which we are able to incorporate a mindfulness informed by faith into our lives will be inversely proportionate to the negative impact of undirected anger in our lives. More faith equals less resentment and anger. When we find we are getting bogged down by details and frustrations, after first taking steps to manage angry reactions, we can direct attention to shifting our attitude to spiritual "truth." This practice will not only assist us in our moment-to-moment management of our thoughts and attitudes, but also in the progressive process of psychic shift to a conscious connection with our Creator. By utilizing faith to engage and process our frustrations, we also develop our faith, and our capacity for faithful trust. Like developing and building any muscle, the more we utilize faith and the more challenging the "weight" we lift, the stronger our faith becomes.

CHAPTER 20

Seeing through the Creator's Eyes

IN THE PAST few chapters, we defined anger as having two primary causes:

- Nullification of one's will
- Infringement on one's honor

Then we separated anger into two categories:

- Anger that emerges out of happenstance, which we labeled as undirected anger/frustration, because it seems to have no "one" to blame
- Anger that has a clear destination, which we labeled as directed anger/frustration, because it is caused by a specific person(s), group, or entity

We discussed how our experience of processing undirected anger can shift as we foster our faith and acceptance of the purposefulness and divine direction of our lives. As we develop mindfulness of our Creator's ever presence, we become more and more able to view circumstances we encounter as part of a broader plan. In fact, if we break it down, our "undirected anger" is a subtle, often undetected, anger toward our Creator. Processing this anger actually represents an opportunity to improve our relationship with our Creator, achieving a powerful acceptance and forgiveness. Yet, even more powerful is the reverse influence this sort of exercise can have on the quality of our faith. By utilizing faith as a tool to overcome resentment, we become more G-d-conscious, and our faith becomes more meaningful. Engaging faith in relation to our disappointments works like a self-sharpening knife. As we harness faith to face frustration, our conscious faith grows; as our conscious faith grows, our ability to harness faith to face frustration likewise develops.

In this chapter, we will expand the reach of this tool and demonstrate how a program of conscious contact can help us remove the destructive impact of directed anger/frustration, while simultaneously enhancing and expanding our spirituality and G-d-consciousness.

At first glance, this seems difficult to accept. Viewing happenstance in our lives—such as flat tires and the like—as part of a purposeful cosmic plan, is reasonable. We can make sense of a divine role in happenstance by conceding that there may be someone "pulling the strings." But to use this sort of thinking to somehow excuse the freely chosen misbehavior of others seems unjustified.

- How can we earnestly utilize a program of faith and G-d-consciousness as a healthy antidote to anger if some people's actions—and the pain they created—came about through their own free-willed choice?
- How is it fair to blame G-d for such people's bad choices?
- How is it fair to ourselves to let such people off the hook?

The key here is to begin to develop a new way of looking at the world. One can potentially view the world through two lenses:

- Through the eyes of the created
- Through the eyes of the Creator

Through the lens of created beings, this world is a collection of separate entities interacting with one another. When we look at the world, we see people, places, and things. We experience these things as independent entities that we—as independent entities ourselves—interact with.

However, when viewing life through a spiritual lens, there is an elevated way to see ourselves and the world around us. Looking at the world through "G-d lenses" means reflecting on the fact that G-d sees the whole picture. Our Creator sees the world as a continuum from creation until now. G-d is neither confined by time nor space and remains neither changed nor affected by any change in us or in the world.[1] As we reflect upon G-d's existence, we begin to comprehend the meaning of true unity. We can begin to get a glimpse of how everything around us is really part of a broad plan, an exquisite tapestry of interwoven aspects. For the Creator—and for us as spiritual beings trying to view things from the Creator's perspective—everything around us is part of an outflow of creative light that began at the moment of the universe's inception. It is all a continuation of one process and history.

When we look at the world through the lens of separate entities, we see a world of separation. In a world of separation, we see separate entities acting in ways that are unfair or against our will. It is only natural to became frustrated and even angry at these separate entities.

As we begin to practice viewing the world through the Creator's lens, we start to become aware that we aren't just

---

[1] *Tanya*, part 2, "The Gate of Faith and Trust," chap. 7, "As it is written, 'You were [the same] before the world was created, You are [the same] after the world was created,' without any change in His Being, not even in His knowledge…"

interacting with separate entities, we are also interacting with expressions of divine light at the same time. From this perspective, the creation surrounding us is simply the medium and expression of the Creator. This sort of perspective elevates our worldview from material to spiritual and increases our ability to look for the divine in all areas of our life.

When we practice seeing the world through the Creator's lens, we become less anchored to our resentment and anger. We are able to face the hurt and frustration and say, "If other people make bad choices, that's their problem. Yet there is purpose and meaning in how I choose to handle my experience of and reaction to those choices." Each of these circumstances, from the most painful to the most mundane, represent the opportunity for growth and development, ultimately leading us toward self-actualization.

This perspective does not abrogate the need to work to resolve pain and heal traumas. Often, people apply an overly simplistic program of faith and G-d-consciousness to their complex problems, as if it were some sort of magic pill that heals all the pain. This is not true. Healing trauma and pain requires hard work, much time, and often professional help. Our point here is that through an approach of faith and G-d-consciousness, we can open a door to the strength and comfort we need to accept and face the challenges that come our way. When we seek out the healing measures that allow us to address and transcend our painful traumas, help others, and live a happy and fulfilled life, we are acting in faith that this is our Creator's will.

Developing this outlook as a sustained attitude for life has further benefit. When we train our mind's eye to view the world through the unified lens of the Creator, everything around us becomes elevated. Recognizing inherent divinity in everything gives expression to that reality. This not only raises our satisfaction and happiness, it raises everyone and everything around us.[2] When there is nothing that can separate us from our Creator, everything around us—both pleasant and challenging—becomes a vehicle to engage with and experience G-d. This is the true inner principle of living a life of spiritual unity. With this worldview, we don't only connect to G-d through prayer and meditation; life itself becomes a viable conduit for connection. The areas of life that lead to disappointment and pain represent the richest of opportunities to develop and grow our conscious connection.

---

2   Rebbe Nachman of Breslov, *Likutei Moharan* 282, "And by finding the goodness within him and judging him favorably, one brings him to return to the true path of his soul."

CHAPTER 21

Prayer II: A World of Prayer

IN THE PAST few chapters, we discussed the final phase of this six-step process to developing a vibrant conscious connection:

- We discussed how internalizing the acute awareness of the presence and influence of G-d in our lives can be enhanced through the practice of faithful speech, drawing the consciousness of spirituality into every aspect of our lives.
- We explored anger and resentment specifically, reflecting on how awareness of our Creator's influence and presence in all aspects of our lives can act as an antidote to many of the destructive consequences that come along with unmitigated resentment.
- We highlighted how utilizing spiritual tools against the negative outcomes of frustration, like a self-sharpening knife, is itself a powerful exercise that further develops conscious contact.

Let us now discuss entering the "world of prayer."

We have previously discussed the power of prayer as a spiritual practice, as well as the benefits of speaking out spiritual ideas. Now we want to take things further. As our awareness and consciousness of our Creator's presence in our lives comes into sharper focus, a door opens to double down on the "profits" of our effort and really expand our prayerful practice. This is what we mean when we talk about a world of prayer. It is a paradigm shift between the world we once operated in and the world ahead of us. When we live in the world of prayer, we don't have to let days or even hours pass without acknowledging and speaking to our Creator in first person. In this new "world," prayer transitions from being a scheduled ritual to a vibrant and ongoing dialogue with our Creator.

This shift in perspective does not require strenuous effort and self-discipline because, as our conscious connection grows, only constant prayer will do. The more we develop constant awareness of the presence of our Creator, the greater our opportunity and the innate motivation to develop a constant prayer dialogue.

However, the idea of constant prayer may trigger resistance:

- How is it practical?
- What about the other important activities that come along with a vibrant spiritual life?

- What about caring for our families, attending to our jobs, paying the bills, helping others, and even ritual religious prayers and study, all of which require focus? How is this possible if we are busy praying all day?

The key is to remind ourselves that we are only seeking to develop a more potent consciousness of our Creator's presence, and to express that consciousness in speech. As we affirm in our hearts and minds the role of that divine presence in the events of our life, we have a new opportunity for relationship. We can then begin to develop a constant dialogue with our Creator. We can enter a world of prayer. This dialogue doesn't take us away from life; it helps us to jump further into life. The objective is to engage life fully and mindfully through the medium of speech, aware not only of the details going on around us, but also of the presence of G-d within each moment.

It is important to note that speaking out words of prayer is not the only way to practice this discipline. Though the spoken and heard word carries its own unique power, speaking out in dialogue is not always the most practical or meaningful type of prayer. There are two other expressions of prayer that will be useful in creating a world of prayer in our lives:

- Internal dialogue with our Creator. This practice involves talking with G-d in our minds. This can be particularly useful in a crowded room or in the middle of a project. We can just take a moment to draw our minds back to the presence of our Creator and say hello. How often do we "wake up" out of an argument or conversation we're having in our minds with someone who isn't even there? Perhaps we aren't talking to them at all; perhaps every conscious thought is really a conversation with G-d. Maybe we could direct our internal narrative toward being an ongoing dialogue with our Creator in our minds. Whether happy or sad, it's always a good time to check in with our Creator.
- Writing out prayers to or dialogue with our Creator. Many people find it much easier to express themselves and put their thoughts together on paper—why not do that with our Creator? We can write to our Creator as if He is our pen pal. This medium can be very effective because it allows for forethought and enables us to calmly gather and process our feelings so we can formulate what we want to say.

These two forms of expression are extremely powerful and meaningful. Though they may be utilized in some of the prayer exercises we mentioned earlier, they are most practical here when seeking to build a world of prayer in and around our lives. When an ongoing dialogue is all that will do, engaging prayer through multiple mediums becomes not only practical but necessary.

As we continue to progress, and we develop a sense of comfort in the world of prayer, we are less and less separated from G-d-consciousness. Everything we do, we do with our Creator. Every activity further builds and engenders deep connectedness. We can continue to live with a deep and meaningful sense that our Creator is right there with us.

STEP 6: G-D IS IN CHARGE—ENCOUNTERING G-D IN REAL LIFE

Step 6 was about getting real about faith and the reality of our lives. We saw that this means having a mature conversation about faith in a Creator Who created a world that has pain, sadness, and disappointment. This process began with exercises to develop a more constant awareness that every aspect of our life is an expression of G-d's will. We started by establishing these concepts in our consciousness through continued practice of daily meditation and consistent mindfulness. We partnered these efforts with the practice of spiritual speech, verbalizing our faithful convictions as a mantra and prayer, which will act to transfer our theoretical and intellectual beliefs to our hearts.

In order to address these two areas fully and be honest in real time about how we feel about what is going on in our lives, we turned our attention to our anger and resentment. We realized that we need to uncover how our feelings interact with the idea that our Creator is in charge of everything, or at the very least, allows everything that occurs. We saw that this part cannot be ignored because increased awareness of our Creator's active role in the painful parts of our lives leads to a natural and inevitable frustration. We also pointed out that we are not seeking to use faith to superficially gloss over our frustrations. An attitude of mature faith demands that we acknowledge the painful impact of others on our lives and the feelings that emerge from them, while also affirming that there is purpose to the experience. The goal here is to get honest and to develop a real relationship. The specific work that we discussed was focusing on how we start the day and on righting our attitudes so that we can approach all challenges and bumps with clarity. This effort will act in turn to sharpen and strengthen our conviction about our Creator's place in our lives.

We began by reflecting on our undirected anger and then our directed anger, acknowledging and moving toward the acceptance that whatever happens, our Creator ultimately allowed it and willed it to be as an expression of infinite kindness. We sought to look at our lives not only through the lens of the created but also through the lens of our Creator, and to look for the unity in all things by acknowledging a purposefulness to it all, even if we don't understand. In doing so, we sought to break free from the myopic perspective that emerges out of the human ego and to see a broader and collective view of things. By practicing this attitude and perspective, we hope to saturate our lives with a sense of true and sustained conscious contact.

We saw how as our conscious connection evolves, we have the opportunity to further and further develop what we have gained. We could begin to live in a world of prayer by continuing a simple and constant dialogue with our Creator in all aspects of our lives. This practice can fill our lives with the constant awareness of the presence of our Creator, and the knowledge that He is our constant companion in our spiritual journey. This is conscious contact. A spirituality that is real, practical, and that fills our lives with meaning, purpose, and fulfillment.

Into Action—Step 6: G-d Is in Charge

THOUGHT, SPEECH, ACTION

Practice #1: Thought

We will begin the exercises of Step 6 in the same way as the previous steps: by focusing on our conscious thoughts. Here we will focus in on the active presence of our Creator in our lives. As before, our goal is to transform cold and removed ideas into an internally vibrant experiential awareness. As we said earlier, this operation entails a two-part discipline:

- The first relies on meditative thought: simple acknowledgments throughout the day, as well as more intensive reflection at certain designated times.
- The second will be discussed in the next chapter and relates to how we utilize speech to process ideas and establish them in our minds.

Let us begin by illustrating what the practice of meditative thought exercises in this area might look like in relation to our Creator's active presence and involvement in our lives. As we discussed in the fifth step, we can begin with the things we see around us. In Step 5, we discussed utilizing questions to open the mind and engage our calculative, sometimes agnostic, thoughts. We will utilize these here as well.

We will begin our meditation by identifying an aspect of our lives and then asking ourselves, "How did this person, place, thing, or situation come to be in my life?" We could begin with the house or structure we are currently in. We would ask, "Who lives here? Myself and my family. Who decided that these people should be my family? How is it that this specific person is my life partner and spouse? While I believe this person is my soulmate, how likely was it that I would meet my soulmate at just the right time and place to allow our marriage to be a reality? It's nearly impossible that through my own ingenuity, charisma, or wisdom *alone* I came to marry this person. It's perfectly plausible that this was divinely inspired. If that is true, then all the causations and derivatives of that union, both biological and circumstantial, were influenced by my Creator's guidance over my life and journey. Perhaps everything I have—my children and my life circumstances—are gifts from G-d… And back to the house and neighborhood that I live in. It may be that G-d chose my spouse and the repercussions of that reality, but surely I myself chose to live here? I went and looked at many homes, and my spouse and I chose this one…Yet, perhaps that's not entirely true either. Perhaps G-d also influenced this…perhaps G-d placed me here for a purpose, to fulfill a mission, to be a channel for his love, at this specific place, at this specific time?"

As we practice this, we can take a few moments to think deeply about the power of this idea and let the wave of realization wash over us that everything—every single detail in our lives—is the will of our Creator. We may feel like we don't *know* this at the level of fact, but let's remember that this is not a philosophical exercise. Doubts or limitations of faith are normal for anyone. In this process, we are seeking the experience of connection with our Creator—the kind that can permeate every facet of our lives. That becomes viable as we allow ourselves to ponder the plausible reality that there is a Creator of the universe, that that Creator formed us, and being an all-powerful presence, He instituted and influenced every aspect of our lives. We can begin by just pondering what it might feel like to know with certainty that those statements are true and how electric that might feel. This kind of reflection opens the door to a powerful and thrilling experience of faith—the acceptance that our Creator is actually there, actually cares, and is really present.

After we experience some level of conscious awareness of G-d's presence through these meditations, we can couple this time of deep meditation with the practice of constant mindfulness. By making this attitude a part of our constant reality, we transform these from being fleeting thoughts to existential awareness—to the realm of our *now*. We practice consistently bringing into our minds the possibility that G-d is actively present and that we are never alone. With this sort of tool, every detail of our lives becomes a vehicle to experience connection with our Creator—a truly vibrant and conscious connection and faith.

Practice #2: Speech

The second type of meditation we utilize in Step 6 is the spiritual tool of speech. What this really means is to utilize all types of speech, from the spoken to the written, as an adjunct to meditation, allowing these concepts to be embedded in the deepest parts of our selves. We previously discussed the tool of spiritual speech and identified it as critical to the process of incorporating faith and awareness of our Creator's active role and presence in our lives. We discussed incorporating simple faithful phrases into our regular speech but acknowledged that the impact of these alone may be limited and somewhat superficial. The more intensive and powerful version of spiritual speech is entering a world of prayer—learning how to develop an ongoing dialogue with our Creator.

Let's use some examples to illustrate what we mean. We will utilize the "for the sake of heaven" attitude we developed in Step 2 of this process. We will focus on how we are already doing much good in our lives, as well as developing the right intention behind that good.

Imagine we are on our way to a house of worship or some sort of spiritual gathering. We could start the trip by speaking to our Creator in the following way: "G-d (or whichever semantic meets your conviction as a reference to our Creator), I am on my way to _____. I am going as an expression of love and devotion to You. [Creator,] in this process, please assist me in living up to our ideal for me—to be kind, loving, and compassionate. May it be Your will that I show all the people I meet along the way the acceptance and love that I believe You have for me."

Once we are there, and as we engage life, we might lose focus or deviate from our ideal behavior and/or attitude. We can immediately pause and say a short prayer out loud or in our minds: "[Creator,] I lost focus just now. I forgot I was here as an expression of my devotion to Your will. I got busy in my mind competing with those around me, thinking negative or hateful thoughts. I don't want to do that anymore. Please help me refocus myself toward whom You would have me be."

As we leave, we might say a short prayer of thanks: "[Creator,] thanks for this great opportunity. Thank You for coming with me. For always being with me, especially during these intimate spiritual moments. I would love to come back soon, and I would love it if You stayed with me as I go out now and get busy with my day."

When we are on our way to work, we can say: "[Creator,] I'm on my way to the job I am so grateful to have (or to the job I can't wait to replace). I am going to work as an expression of my commitment to my family, to engage in life, and to utilize my strengths to better the world around me. [Creator,] please assist me in showing kindness to the people I meet along the way and to conduct myself with honesty and truth. My hope is to be a fine example to all those around me—those who work for me and those I work for—of Your love."

Then, during the day, especially when we find ourselves burnt out, or after a tense conversation: "[Creator,] I just lost my cool, I'm feeling burnt out. I don't want to treat people that way. I don't believe You want me to. Can You help me? I have faith that You placed these people or situations in my life for a reason, and that facing this will help me to grow or accomplish some sort of meaningful mission. I hope to remain mindful that You are with me in all the challenging interactions ahead."

Finally, when we leave work: "[Creator,] wow, that was a tough day. Thank You for being with me. Thank You for my successes. Please help me to do even better tomorrow. I want to invite You to join me as I head home."

These are just examples of the types of personal prayer we can practice. Formal prayers are wonderful and important, but additional private prayers can really enhance our connectedness. We encourage the reader to fashion their prayers according to their own conviction and faith. The same can be applied to any activity we engage. Start with a simple prayer of mindfulness, setting the right mood and attitude, and by affirming the intention, goal, and mission. In the middle, pause—especially when things get off track—and check in or ask for help. Lastly, when you complete your task, invite in gratitude and thankfulness. All of this can be spoken or journaled. The key is to be positive and forward-minded.

Action: An Epilogue

WE NOW COME to the end of our journey. We have spent a lot of time talking about and practicing reflection and prayer. We evaluated the purpose of our lives and of our spiritual efforts. We developed the drive and hope to succeed in our spiritual quest and the willingness to follow through. We chose to engage a spiritual process of growth. We reintroduced ourselves to our Creator, to the world around us, and even to ourselves. We invited a perspective of G-d into every aspect of our lives. All that's left now is to carry this energy outward.

One of the great Chassidic masters of the nineteenth century was Rabbi Menachem Mendel Morgenstern, the Rebbe of Kotzk, known especially for his insightful and incisive sayings that always seem to cut directly to the point at hand. There is one story of the Kotzker (as he is known) that perfectly captures the essence of what we have been talking about until now. There are two parts to the story, but both strive to answer the very same question: Where is G-d?

The story goes that young Menachem Mendel was once challenged by his father with this question: "Mendel," his father said, "where is G-d? If you can tell me, I will give you a gold coin."

"Where is G-d?" Mendel responded. "Father, I'll give you two gold coins if you can tell me where He isn't."

The next story takes place much later in Menachem Mendel's life, when he was already a leader of thousands of followers. His students approached him and asked, "Great Rebbe, exalted spiritual teacher, can you tell us where we can find G-d?" The Kotzker looked at his students and said, "Where is G-d, you ask? Wherever you let Him in."

This is the essence of the journey we have been taking. We began with a desire for conscious connection. The normal assumption is that any growth entails taking on or bringing in something new. Yet here we found that growth and development require waking up to what is already here, to developing a consciousness of the vibrant connection that flows through every aspect of our lives. We have gained the mindful awareness that our Creator is everywhere we look *and* waiting for us in the last place we might have thought to look—in our hearts. We came to the realization that everything we had searched for outside of ourselves was waiting for us right at "home" the whole time.

Action: An Epilogue

What will it take, then, to make all this real? Action.

Spiritual concepts are wonderful. Thinking about them feels hopeful, sharing them with others is exhilarating...but on their own, they won't last. To really effect change, we must take action. The action starts with the right thoughts and a healthy attitude, but it will always continue by acting on our faith. For some, this may mean connecting more to religious practice, while for others it may mean more studying and learning of religious and/or spiritual texts. It may mean acting on the spirituality we gain in our lives and sharing what we have learned with others. For most, it will mean a combination of the above.

A relationship with our Creator is complex. Relationships mean love, they mean respect, and they require a measure of discipline and surrender. What we have looked to establish is a foundation—a beginning upon which a meaningful relationship with our Creator, as you understand G-d, can be further developed and built. We want to build a healthy foundation upon which spiritual development can be both sincere and balanced. Where you go from here is up to you. The beauty of developing conscious contact, of embracing our relationship with our Creator, is that we become active and adult participants in our spiritual journey. Being an adult participant means formulating and holding opinions, but also asking for guidance when necessary. It means owning responsibility and opportunity. More than anything, it means embracing the responsibility and opportunity for giving to and influencing others.

This is what we mean by action. As we reach the end of this process, the Into Action practices ask of us: What will *you* do with this? How will your relationship with G-d flow outward from your heart and into your life and to those you love?

That we leave to you, with the hope that someday we will meet as we all travel the path of spiritual destiny.

Notes

Notes

About the Author

MENACHEM POZNANSKI, a licensed clinical social worker and author, has worked in the field of substance abuse prevention, addictions treatment, and recovery support for twenty years. Since 2004, Mr. Poznanski has served as director of The Living Room (TLR), a division of Our Place in NY, Inc. TLR is a clubhouse program for Jewish young adults and couples in recovery from addictions. Menachem is co-author of *Stepping Out of the Abyss: A Jewish Guide to the Twelve Steps* (Mosaica Press 2017) and editor at The Light Revealed and Consciously, two social media publishers focused on youth and the messages of Jewish spirituality. Menachem received his master's degree in social work from the Yeshiva University Wurzweiler School of Social Work and lives in Cedarhurst, NY, with his wife, Naomi, and their children, Zoe and Tani.

Also from this author

STEPPING OUT OF THE ABYSS

The twelve-step philosophy identifies spirituality as the core element of alcoholism and addiction. The principles of the twelve-step program have produced a freedom from suffering for millions, catapulting them into the serenity of a sober life. Through practice of the twelve steps, they receive a set of spiritual tools for achieving mastery over their problems.

This unique, important, and easy-to-read volume is full of information, tools, stories, and inspiration. It dispels misconceptions and helps the reader—whether someone struggling with addiction or addictive behavior, family member, clergyman, mental health professional, or other concerned member of the community—understand how to use the twelve steps.

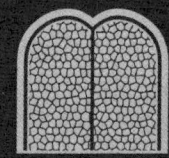

MOSAICA PRESS
BOOK PUBLISHERS
Elegant, Meaningful & Bold

info@MosaicaPress.com
www.MosaicaPress.com

The Mosaica Press team of acclaimed editors and designers is attracting some of the most compelling thinkers and teachers in the Jewish community today. Our books are available around the world.

HARAV YAACOV HABER
RABBI DORON KORNBLUTH